HOW IT WORKS

OCEANS

STEPHEN HALL

award

Series editor: Elizabeth Miles
Additional research: Ivailio Grigorov
Cover design: Duck Egg Blue
Illustrations: Jim Channell, David Hardy, Sebastian Quigley,
Steve Seymour, Steve Weston and Gerald Witcomb
Photography: Shutterstock.com (Andrey Nosik, Anna segeren, aquapix, bcampbell65, Choksawatdikorn, davemhuntphotography, David Thyberg, De Visu, DWeeks, Four Oaks, Francois BOIZOT, gabrisigno, JonMilnes, Malbert, Mikado767, Napat, nartt, Nattapon Ponbumrungwong, Nick Kashenko, Off Axis Production, Oleg Kovtun Hydrobio, opsorman, OutdoorWorks, photomatz, Ricado Castro, Richard Whitcombe); NASA/GSFC; S.clarkorbital (CC BY-SA 4.0)

ISBN 978-1-78270-004-3

Copyright © Award Publications Limited

All rights reserved. No part of this publication may be reproduced or utilised in any form or by any means electronic or mechanical, including photocopying, recording, or by any information storage and retrieval system now known or hereafter invented, without the prior written permission of the publisher.

This edition first published 2025

Published by Award Publications Limited,
The Old Riding School, Welbeck,
Worksop, S80 3LR

/awardpublications   @award.books
www.awardpublications.co.uk

23-1100 1

Printed in China

Contents

The Ocean Floor	6	Submersibles	28
Tides	8	Shipwrecks	30
Waves and Wind	10	Ocean Life	32
Coastlines	12	Coastal Life	34
Frozen Seas	14	Seabirds	36
Mapping the Sea	16	Coral Reefs	38
Early Ships	18	Ocean Pollution	40
Modern Ships	20	Mining the Sea	42
Fishing	22	Ocean Power	44
Submarines	24	Index	46
Scuba Diving	26		

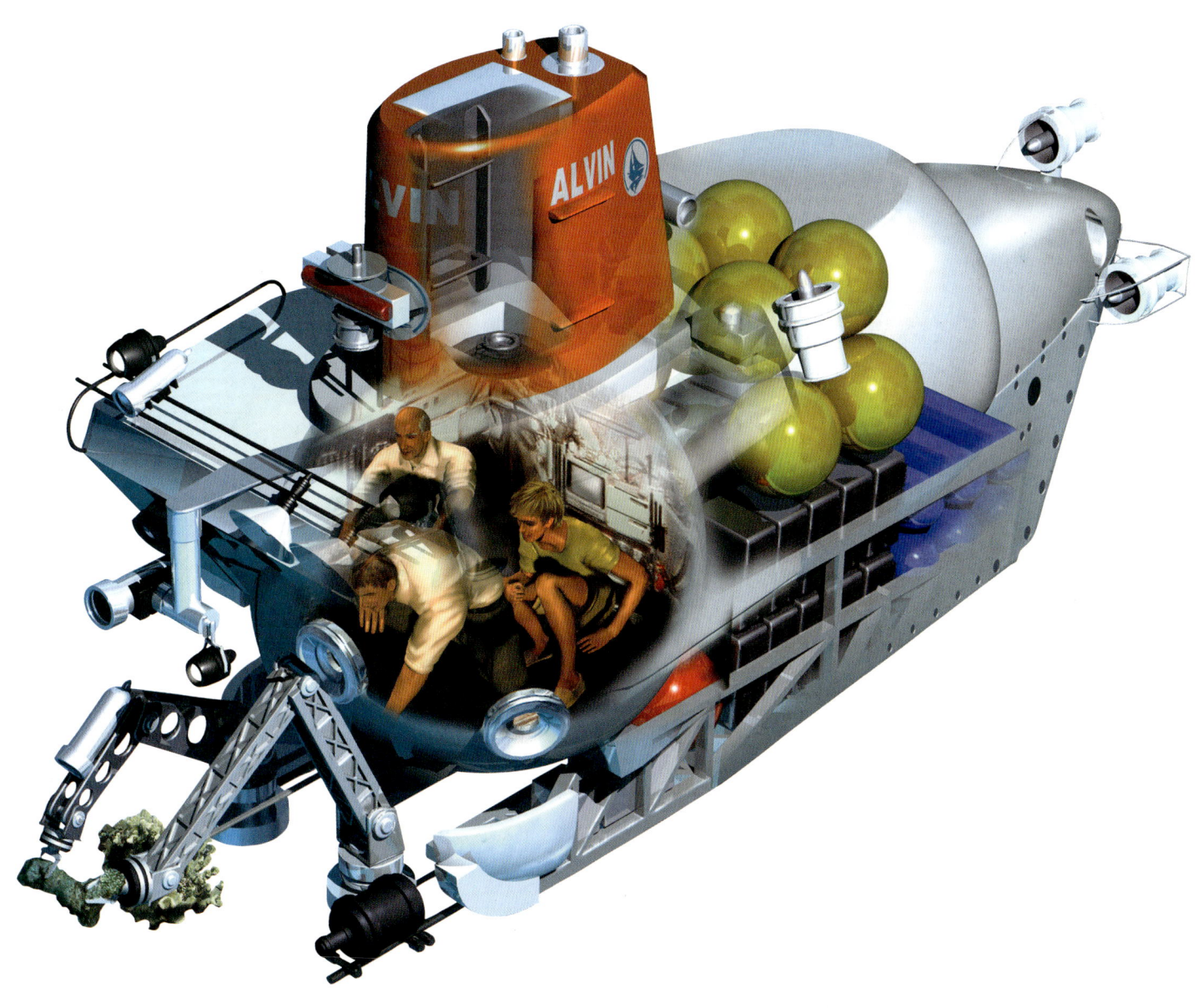

The Ocean Floor

The Earth's thin surface layer is known as the crust. It is split into several pieces, called plates, that drift very slowly on a lower layer of molten, denser rock. Two types of rock form these plates: continental and oceanic. Continental rock is about 40 kilometres thick, increasing to 70 kilometres under high mountain ranges. Oceanic rock is much thinner – it is only about 6 kilometres thick. Beneath the oceans, new oceanic rock is continuously forming at 'spreading ridges' where plates are pulling apart. Oceanic rock is also continuously being destroyed in 'subduction zones', where it dips under a continental plate and melts.

Water fills up the great oceanic basins, but the amount of water varies over time. Today, sea levels are high enough to cover the lower-lying parts of the continents. These submerged parts are called continental shelves.

As mountains are worn down by the weather, material is carried by rivers into the ocean

The edge of the continental shelf slopes down to the deep ocean floor

Low-lying land is flooded by the ocean when sea levels rise

Molten rock rises and then sets hard to form the core of mountains

Oceanic crust sometimes continues below the thicker continental crust

The birth of an ocean

Volcanic activity starts when hot rock breaks through the Earth's crust (*left, top*). As the crust splits and two or more plates drift apart, a steep-sided valley is formed, like the Rift Valley of East Africa (*middle*). The valley floods, and over millions of years widens into an ocean (*bottom*). Long ago, Africa and America split apart and the Atlantic Ocean filled the gap.

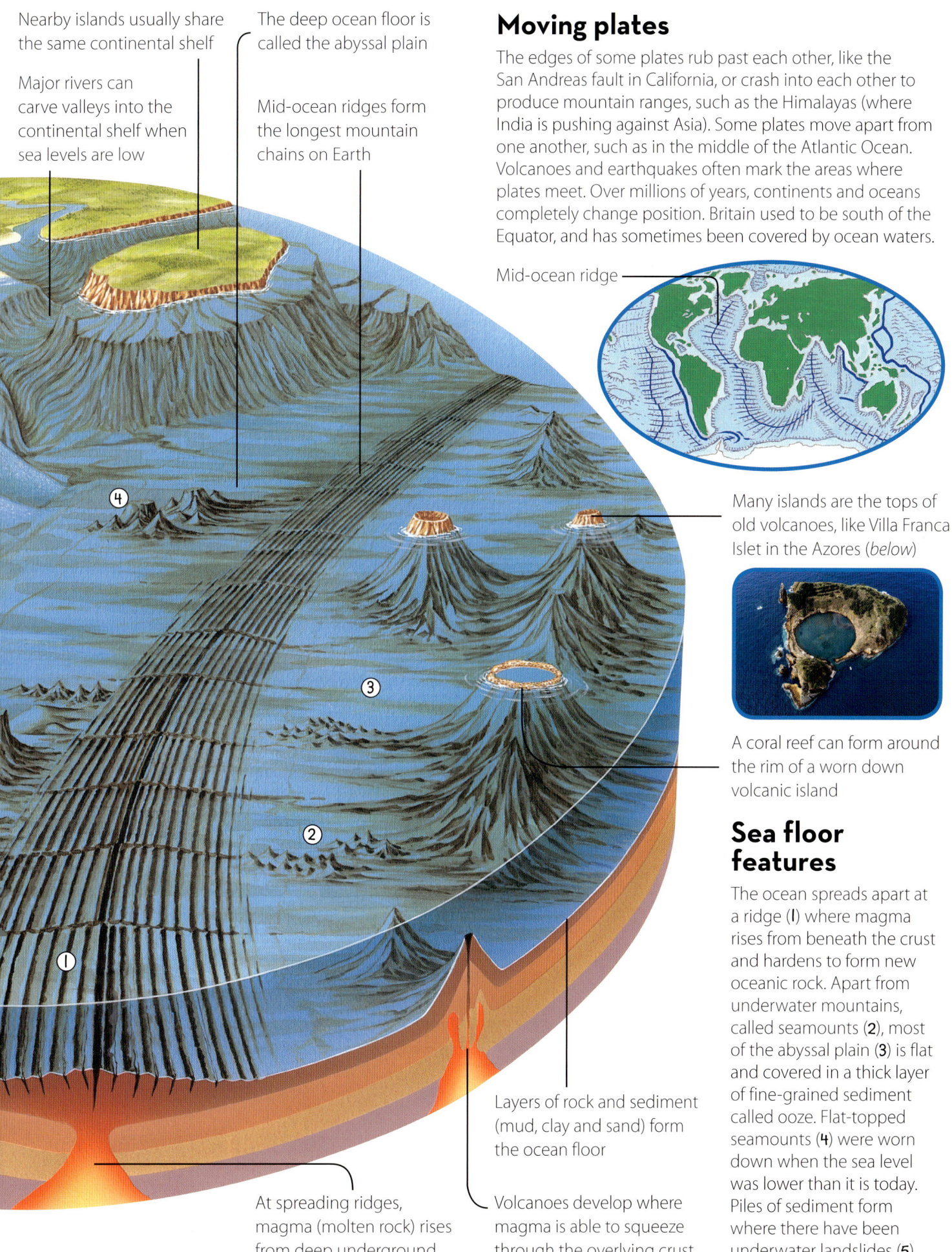

Nearby islands usually share the same continental shelf

Major rivers can carve valleys into the continental shelf when sea levels are low

The deep ocean floor is called the abyssal plain

Mid-ocean ridges form the longest mountain chains on Earth

Moving plates

The edges of some plates rub past each other, like the San Andreas fault in California, or crash into each other to produce mountain ranges, such as the Himalayas (where India is pushing against Asia). Some plates move apart from one another, such as in the middle of the Atlantic Ocean. Volcanoes and earthquakes often mark the areas where plates meet. Over millions of years, continents and oceans completely change position. Britain used to be south of the Equator, and has sometimes been covered by ocean waters.

Mid-ocean ridge

Many islands are the tops of old volcanoes, like Villa Franca Islet in the Azores (*below*)

A coral reef can form around the rim of a worn down volcanic island

Sea floor features

The ocean spreads apart at a ridge (**1**) where magma rises from beneath the crust and hardens to form new oceanic rock. Apart from underwater mountains, called seamounts (**2**), most of the abyssal plain (**3**) is flat and covered in a thick layer of fine-grained sediment called ooze. Flat-topped seamounts (**4**) were worn down when the sea level was lower than it is today. Piles of sediment form where there have been underwater landslides (**5**).

At spreading ridges, magma (molten rock) rises from deep underground

Layers of rock and sediment (mud, clay and sand) form the ocean floor

Volcanoes develop where magma is able to squeeze through the overlying crust

Tides

The Moon orbits (travels around) the Earth, and together the Earth and Moon orbit the Sun. As this happens, the gravitational forces of the Moon and Sun pull on the oceans, causing tides. The Moon has a more powerful effect on the tides because it is much closer to the Earth. It stretches the Earth's ocean waters into an oval shape, creating a tidal bulge on each side of the Earth. These tidal bulges are where high tides occur.

The usual tidal range – the difference between water levels at high and low tide– is 2–3 metres on open coastlines. Many things can affect the tidal range, including severe weather, the presence of land such as islands, friction of the tide against the sea floor and wind direction. Complicated multiple tides can also occur when different tidal cycles affect one another. The largest tidal ranges are where the shape of the coastline strengthens the tidal effects. Seas that are enclosed, such as the Mediterranean Sea, show a much smaller tidal range than the open oceans.

The effects of the Sun and Moon

Below you can see how the oceans bulge outward towards the Moon and Sun (the effects are exaggerated in the pictures to make them clearer). When the Moon and Sun are at right angles (*pictures* 1 *and* 3) you can see the stronger pull of the Moon on the oceans. Because the Sun is pulling from a different direction the tidal bulges are less extreme and 'neap' tides occur. When the Moon and Sun are in line, their forces combine and more extreme 'spring' tides occur (2 *and* 4). The greatest tides occur during the spring and autumn equinoxes, when the Sun is directly over the Equator and most closely aligned with the Moon. Many plants and animals are adapted to take advantage of tidal ranges.

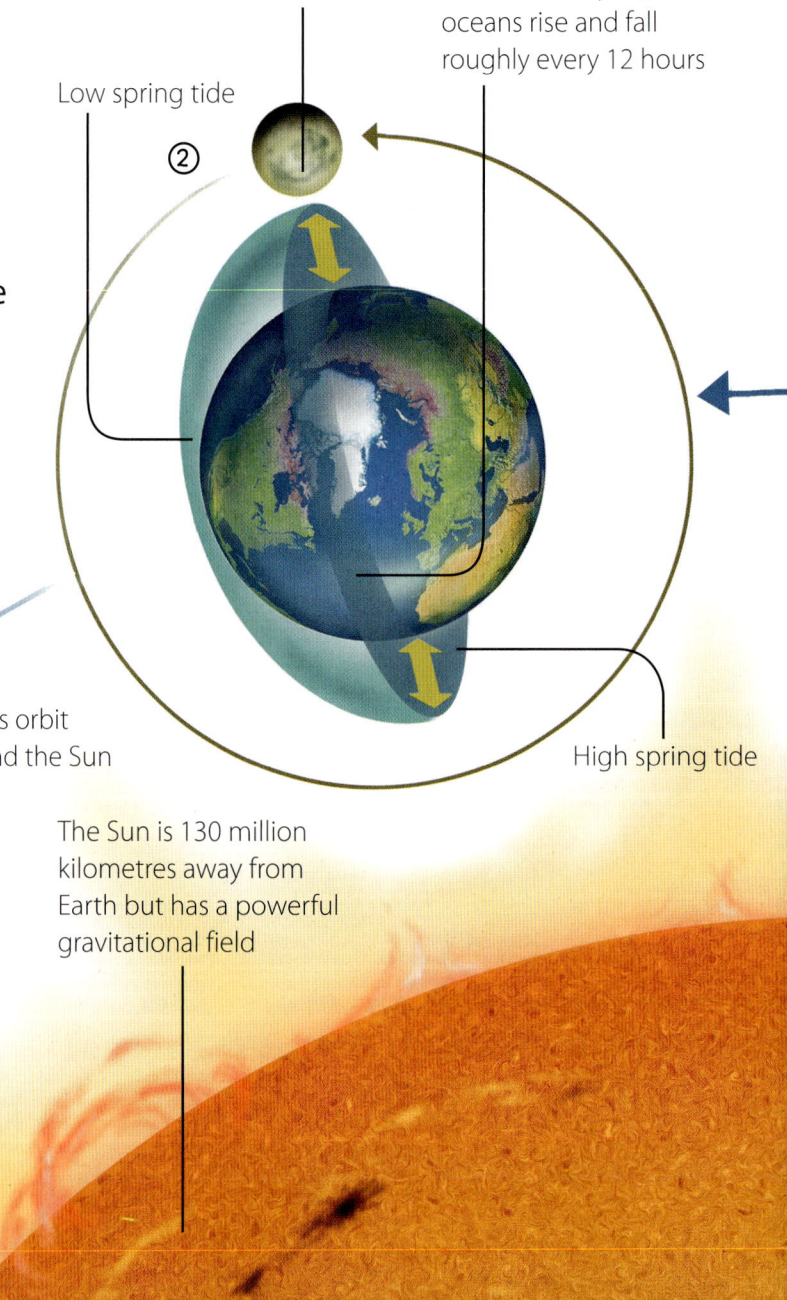

Low neap tide | Low spring tide | High neap tide | High spring tide

Tidal range and plant growth

Because of the regular rise and fall of the oceans, plants and animals live at particular heights along the shoreline. Only salt-resistant lichens live in the splash zone. To stay alive, green seaweed and barnacles need to be low enough to get a covering of water at high tide.

Tidal ranges

The positions of the boat and views of the Moon show the differences between spring and neap tides. At full and new Moon, we get spring tides, when the tidal difference is large. At half Moon, the tidal difference is smaller.

Lichens live above the high tide mark, in the splash zone

High tide waters reach green seaweed, limpets and barnacles

Brown seaweed lives near the low tide mark, so it is underwater most of the time

Red seaweed often grows below the low tide mark

Half Moon visible from Earth

③

The tidal range of a spring tide is larger because the Sun and Moon pull in the same direction

④

The tidal range of a neap tide is smaller because the Sun, Earth and Moon are at right angles

Crescent or new Moon visible from Earth

Waves and Wind

The Earth is like a huge spinning ball, with a heat lamp – the Sun – shining over the Equator. At the Equator, ocean waters become warmer and move out towards the extreme northern and southern parts of the Earth (the North and South poles). At the poles, which are further from the Sun, the water becomes cooler and flows back towards the Equator to begin the cycle again. This is how currents of water move deep in the oceans. Surface currents are caused by winds, the rotation of the Earth, and the position of land masses (*see below, right*).

Winds also cause waves as they blow across the surface of the sea. As shown below, the water itself does not move forward in a wave. The water particles only go round in a circle. Instead, it is the energy that this movement makes that moves forward with a wave.

The Beaufort Scale

The Beaufort Wind Force Scale describes the strength of the wind at sea or on land using numbers from 0 to 12. It relies on signs that can be seen with the eye, rather than on scientific instruments..

0 calm, sea like a mirror
1 light air, small ripples
2 light breeze, small wavelets
3 gentle breeze, wave crests begin to break
4 moderate breeze, small waves and some 'white horses'
5 fresh breeze, frequent waves, many 'white horses'
6 strong breeze, large waves 3 metres high begin to form
7 near gale, rough sea with spray
8 gale, waves up to 6 metres high
9 strong gale, rough waves, up to 9 metres high
10 storm, poor visibility, waves up to 12 metres high
11 violent storm, sea covered in foam, small ships lost to view between wave crests
12 hurricane, waves over 14 metres high, air filled with foam/spray

A well-maintained and professionally crewed ship can withstand violent storms

Waves over 30 metres high have been recorded

Wave peaks are whipped into foam by a strong force 8 gale

In a force 11 storm the sea is covered in foam

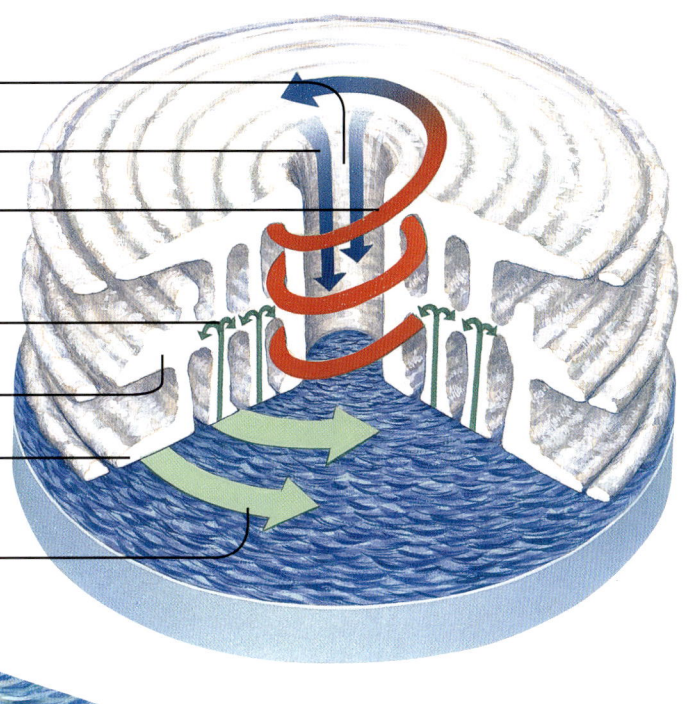

The 'eye' of the storm
Cool, descending air
Air spirals in towards the 'eye' of storm
Warm, rising air
Thunderclouds
Walls of dense cloud
Wind speeds reach over 150 km/h below the storm

Light breezes cause small wavelets

At the end of each wave, water particles are back where they started

As wave height increases, the crests become taller and sharper

In a force 8 gale waves are up to 6 metres high

Deep below a wave the circular motion of the water particles is smaller

The Equator is an imaginary line around the Earth, lying halfway between the poles

The water particles in the wave move in a circular pattern, but the energy of the wave moves forwards

Great storms

Tropical revolving storms (known as typhoons, hurricanes or cyclones) form over warm water and can reach 560–800 kilometres in diameter. Walls of dense cloud form rings around the centre of the storm as warm, moist air is drawn in and spirals rapidly upwards. The 'eye' (centre) of the storm is a calm area of cool, descending air. These storms cause tremendous damage if they pass over land, but soon die out as they move further inland.

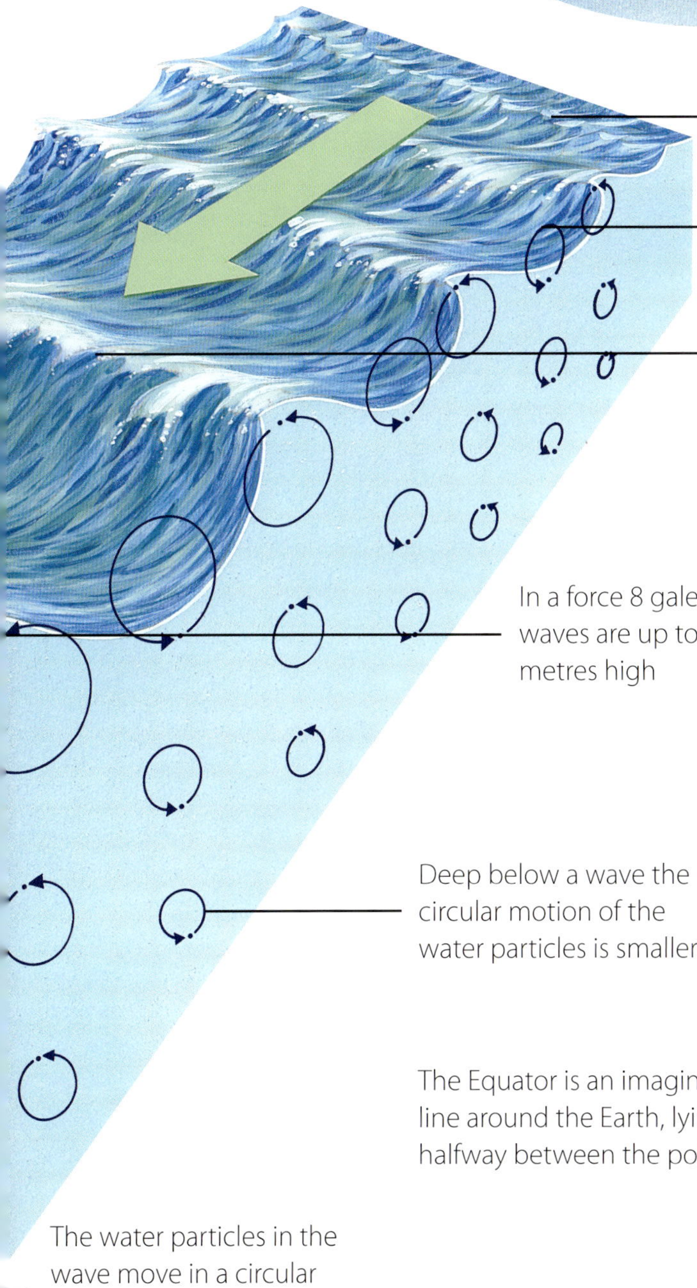

Surface waters

The colours on the map below show the temperatures of land and ocean surface waters. The temperatures are measured by satellites in orbit around the Earth. Warm Equatorial temperatures are shown in orange; cooler polar temperatures are shown in green and blue.

The arrows on the map show the flow of surface ocean currents (warm currents are in red; cold are in blue). These wind driven currents are swung to one side by the rotation of the Earth, creating large circular currents in the oceans. All oceans are connected by currents at various depths. The currents have a great effect on climate. For example, warm waters from the Indian Ocean enter the Atlantic and move north, helping to keep northern Europe warm.

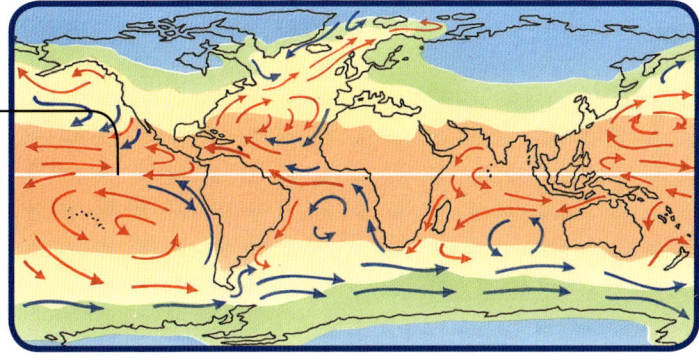

Coastlines

Coasts are where the land and sea do battle. Without human intervention, the sea usually wins. The coastal land that survives the pounding of waves best is made of hard, volcanic rock; soft sandstone, on the other hand, is easily worn away. The slope of coastal rock and any weaknesses in it also influences the shape of the coastline.

Coasts are often popular places for people to live, work and go on holiday. To preserve rapidly eroding coastlines, engineers build sea defences, such as walls of concrete or stone. Beaches are sometimes preserved with walls or breakwaters called groynes. In some countries, whole areas of low-lying land have been reclaimed from the sea by building walls called dykes and then pumping away the sea water.

Large rivers can help to preserve the coast. As they enter the sea, they deposit many tonnes of mud, stone and sand onto the sea floor, building up natural sea defences.

Speed of erosion

How long can a coastline last? There are several things to take into account. In particular, the hardness of the rock, the ferocity of the sea and the presence of sea defences are critical factors.

Over many years, sea levels change, and this also affects how coastlines are eroded (worn down). For example, thousands of years ago, some areas of land were covered by thick sheets of ice that eventually melted. After the weight of the ice was gone, the land slowly rose. This accounts for the ancient beaches found high above the present sea level in many places. Where rock under a coastline is now sinking, the sea can flood areas that were once dry land.

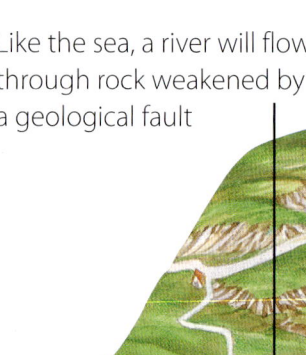

Sand dunes form in sheltered areas

Coves are formed when the sea opens a gap through a neck of hard rock into softer rock behind

Like the sea, a river will flow through rock weakened by a geological fault

Abandoned houses are lost from a rapidly eroding cliff

Rocky debris will soon be ground down into sand by waves

Coastal waves

Waves become shorter and steeper as they approach the coast. This is because the circular motion of water particles within the wave gets pushed upwards by the rising of the sea floor as it gets closer to the coast. Once it reaches its maximum height, the wave breaks. The water then sweeps back out to sea as backwash.

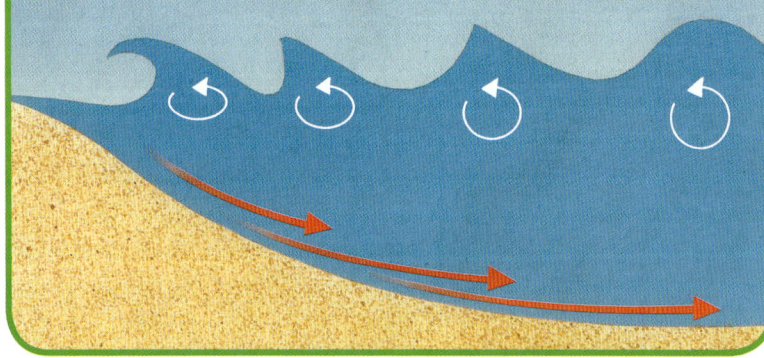

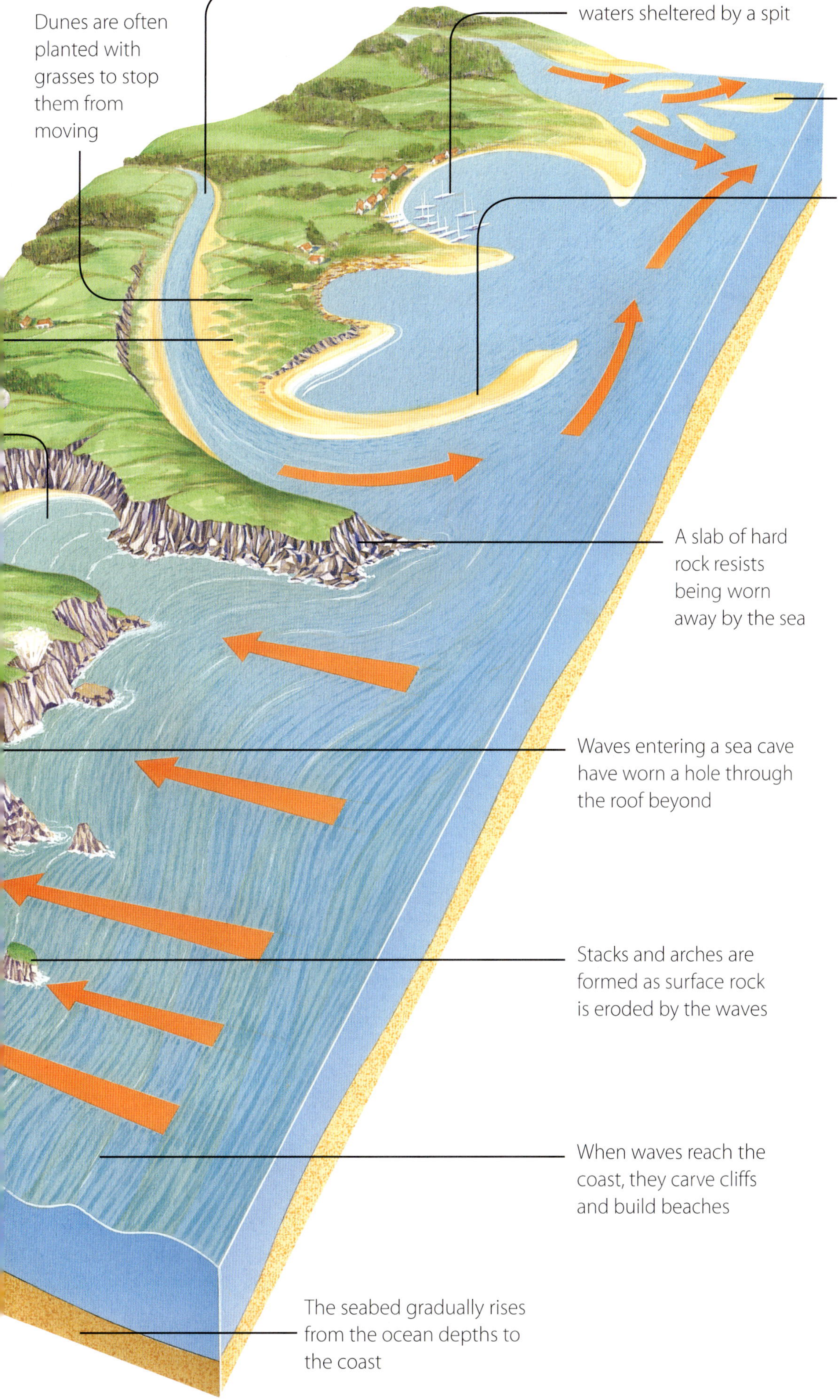

Dunes are often planted with grasses to stop them from moving

A river carries mud, stone and sand out to sea

Boats can anchor safely in waters sheltered by a spit

Sandbars will form offshore if the current is slow

A spit is formed from sand deposited by the river

A slab of hard rock resists being worn away by the sea

Waves entering a sea cave have worn a hole through the roof beyond

Stacks and arches are formed as surface rock is eroded by the waves

When waves reach the coast, they carve cliffs and build beaches

The seabed gradually rises from the ocean depths to the coast

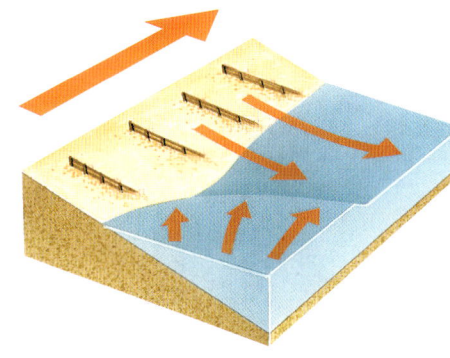

Longshore drift

On coasts, waves move sand and shingle along in a zigzag pattern called longshore drift. Groynes (walls or breakwaters) are sometimes built to slow down this movement and to build up the quantity of sand on beaches.

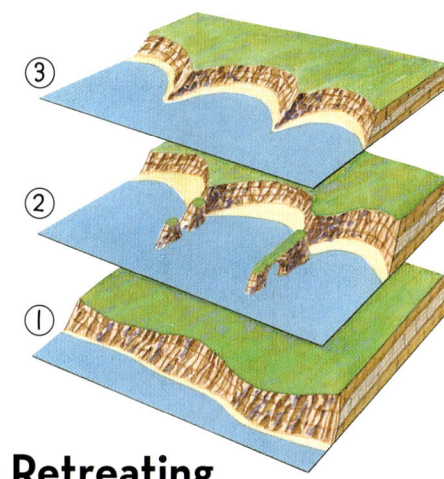

Retreating coasts

Given enough time, waves will erode most coasts (1). Here, soft rock is removed, leaving headlands behind (2). Eventually, these are also worn away (3).

Frozen Seas

The extreme northern and southern regions of our planet are very cold. In the north, the Arctic is an ice-covered ocean bordered by Greenland and the northern continents. Antarctica, in the south, is a huge continent surrounded by the Southern Ocean.

Glaciers (huge masses of moving ice) have built up to form the ice sheets that cover much of Greenland and Antarctica. In places, the ice sheets extend down to the coast and out to sea. Cold winds cause other parts of the sea to freeze, while warmer currents or winds can sometimes melt the sea ice.

Few creatures live on the surface of the frozen seas, but near the edge of the ice there is a rich variety of fish and plankton that provide food for larger animals, such as seals and whales.

Melting ice

Disappearing ice caps cause problems for wildlife, such as polar bears, which are forced to use precious energy swimming between ice floes in order to find food.

Rising warm water melts an area of ice

Icebergs from ice sheets can be large enough to land an aircraft on

Ridges of ice appear where sheets of pack ice bump into each other

The sea begins to freeze, forming 'pancake ice' – these sheets gradually merge together to form pack ice

An icebreaker ploughs through the pack ice

At the boundary with warmer water, the ice edge thins out and gradually disappears

Warm upwelling ocean currents bring nutrients that feed plankton (tiny plants and animals)

For six months of the year the Sun does not rise in the far north or south

Glaciers built up to form the vast Antarctic ice sheet over many years

An ice sheet is formed from snow and ice that has built up over many years and creeps downhill under its own weight

Freezing winds gust out to sea from the ice-covered land

Seasonal changes

During the summer, ice melts at the poles and daylight returns. In the Arctic and Antarctic, the ice edge retreats and the extent of the ice is smaller. In the Arctic, ice seems to be covering a smaller area each summer, and is expected to disappear completely in the summer months by the 2070s. Most scientists believe this is due to global warming.

Greenland is covered by an ice sheet

The summer limits of the pack ice

The winter limits of the pack ice

The limit of icebergs

Antarctica contains over 80 per cent of the world's ice

Ice sheets can extend out to sea for several kilometres

Icebergs (giant lumps of ice) break away from the ice edge in a process called calving, then drift out to sea

When sea water freezes, salt is left behind – the salty water sinks, causing the water to circulate

Warm, less salty water flows up towards the surface where it will cool and freeze, continuing the cycle

Icebergs

Some icebergs break off immense ice sheets and are as large as an island, taking months or even years to melt (1). They are called 'tabular' (table-like) because of their flat tops. Icebergs that break off glaciers are much smaller (2). They carry rocky debris, have a more ragged or angular shape and are mostly found in the Arctic. Nine tenths of an iceberg is underwater. As it melts, it may become unstable and capsize in a spectacular way.

Mapping the Sea

To take measurements of the bottom of an ocean, scientists called oceanographers use sonar (SOund NAvigation and Ranging) because sound waves travel well in water. They measure depth using an echo sounder and build up a picture of the ocean floor using a side-scan sonar system. To find out what the ocean floor is made of, samples of seabed are taken using coring devices. Oceanographers also need to measure the temperature, saltiness and chemistry of the ocean. They use devices that are lowered or towed from research ships and take water samples to analyse in laboratories. Satellites look at an ocean's surface temperature, winds, wave heights and the amount of plankton. Underwater drifting devices and pilotless submarines explore the depths, then transmit their findings back when they surface.

Special radar equipment can look at the oceans even through cloud

Wave heights can be measured by satellite altimeters, which are very accurate, even from a height of 800 kilometres

A bathysonde typically records temperature, salinity (salt content) and pressure

A giant piston corer is used to remove long, deep samples of ocean floor

Towed instruments

An undulator is shaped like a small plane and is towed behind a research ship. It is lowered down to 500 metres below the surface then travels back up, all the time gathering data such as water temperature. A side-scan sonar is also towed. It gathers data to map the shape of the seabed.

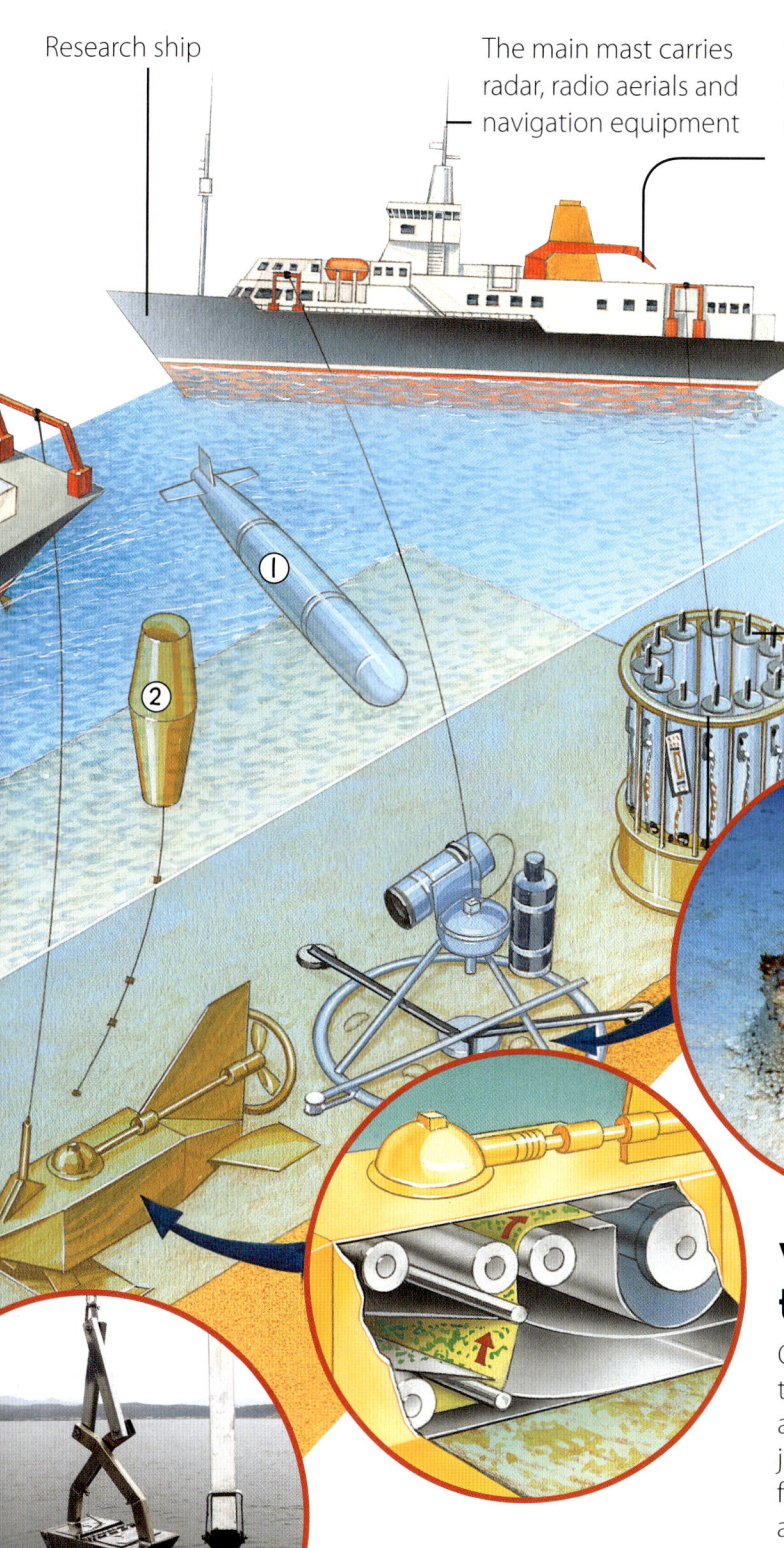

Research ship

The main mast carries radar, radio aerials and navigation equipment

Cranes and supporting frames are fitted so that equipment can be lowered into or raised from the water

Bottles are filled with water at various depths to measure salinity (saltiness)

Research ships

Research ships carry scientists and technicians for weeks at a time to gather information about the ocean. Because these ships are extremely expensive to operate, there are not many of them. Robot explorers like the one pictured left (**1**), are being developed to survey the oceans when ships are not available, or to go on hazardous missions such as exploring under ice caps. Moored buoys (**2**) are left to measure ocean currents and temperature. They send out radio signals so that they can be found again.

What lives at the bottom?

Over 2,000 metres down in the North Atlantic Ocean, a sea cucumber swims just above the ocean floor. Pictures are taken automatically with special time-lapse cameras.

Charts and maps

Computers help produce maps of the sea floor by turning sonar images into three-dimensional pictures. Engineers use the maps to plan where to lay cables and pipelines, or to safely navigate submarines.

Plankton recorder

This device is towed behind ships to measure how much plankton lives near the sea surface. Sea water and plankton enter through the front and a fine silk mesh inside catches the plankton. The plankton are then stored in a cylinder, ready to be analysed later in a laboratory.

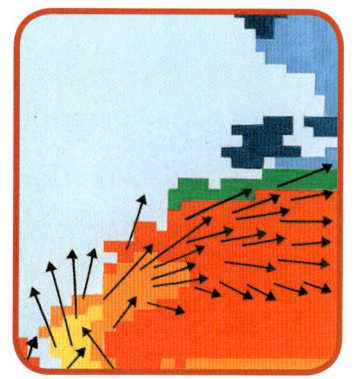

Grab sampler

As its name implies, the grab sampler 'grabs' a sample of the ocean floor and brings it up.

Models

Information about the ocean is fed into special computer programs, called 'models', which can show how the ocean works. Models can help predict the route of accidental oil spills or how the ocean responds to climate change.

17

Early Ships

Until the invention of steam power, the only way ships could move forwards was by using oars or sails. For hundreds of years, wind power enabled explorers to travel all over the oceans, but over the last 200 years sail has given way to other forms of propulsion. Some of the earliest ships relied on oars, or later a combination of oars and sails. The Vikings and Polynesians rowed for days if the wind was not behind them to fill their ships' sails, and ancient Greeks and Romans relied on crews of slaves to row their warships and trading ships.

In the 19th century, steam power started to take over from sails. In shipbuilding, steel began to replace wood, and in the early 20th century oil began to replace coal as fuel. Steam piston engines were replaced by powerful steam turbines, but by the beginning of the 21st century, fuel-efficient marine diesel was the most common power source.

Developments since steam

Ships like *Titanic* were built to cross oceans quickly, carrying businesspeople, immigrants and mail. After the Second World War, aircraft took over these roles, so large passenger ships were used as cruise liners instead. Steam ships were retired because at low speeds diesel engines are cheaper to run. Ships powered by gas turbines (like jet engines) were built from the 1970s but they use a lot of fuel. Today, gas turbines power warships, for which acceleration and speed are important.

Ancient ships

Long-distance voyages were made by the Egyptians in boats made of reeds, palm fibre and tar. Modern recreations have crossed the Atlantic and northern Indian Ocean. Other early ships were built of animal skins and wood. All were used to cross open oceans, but we do not know how many sailors died attempting ocean crossings in such flimsy craft.

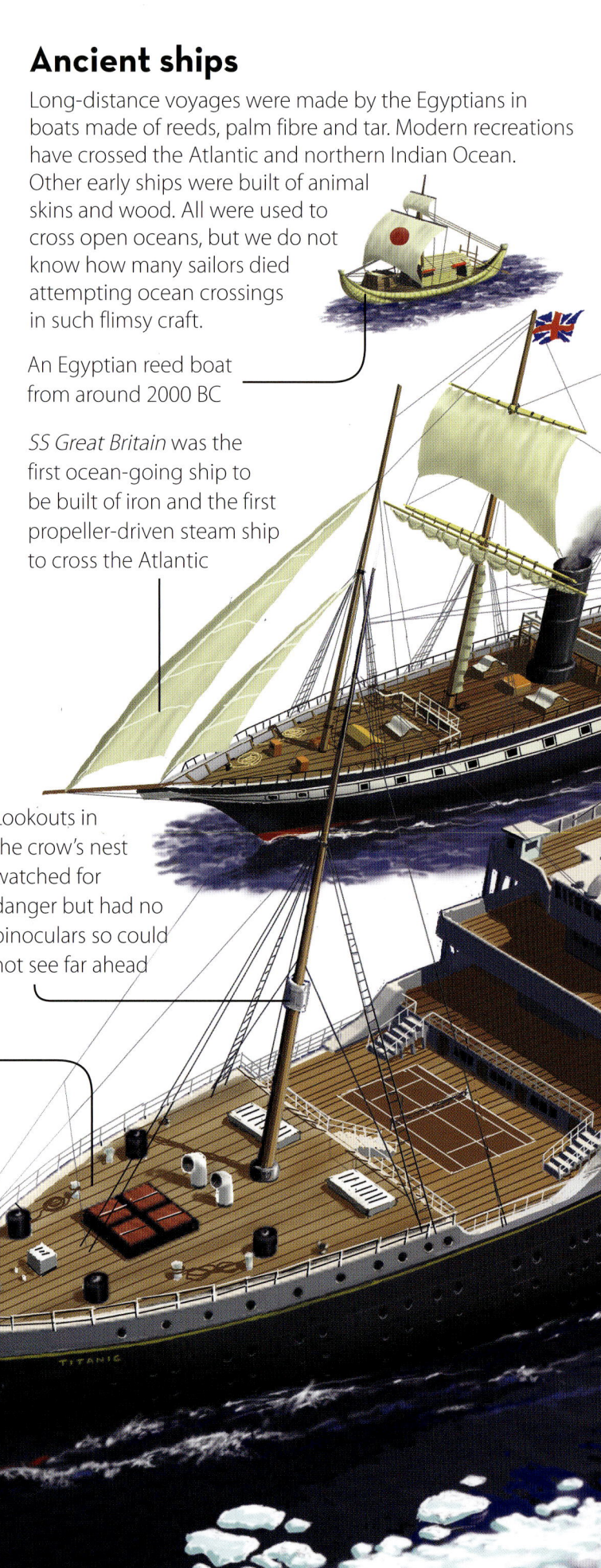

An Egyptian reed boat from around 2000 BC

SS Great Britain was the first ocean-going ship to be built of iron and the first propeller-driven steam ship to cross the Atlantic

Lookouts in the crow's nest watched for danger but had no binoculars so could not see far ahead

Over 1,500 people died when *Titanic* sank on 14 April 1912 after hitting an iceberg

Titanic had three engines (two steam piston engines and one steam turbine engine)

Mayflower carried the Pilgrim Fathers to the New World (America) in 1620

Mayflower was tiny (180 tonnes) and took 63 days to cross the Atlantic

From sail to steam

The development of the sailing ship was slow until about the 15th century, when the Americas began to attract voyagers from the other side of the Atlantic. By the 19th century, the sailing ship had been perfected, but the invention of steam power allowed ships to travel in any direction, whatever the wind. Journeys that had taken months by sail now only took a few weeks to complete.

Three funnels were real; the other was a dummy used for ventilation

Titanic had three propellers and one huge rudder

Titanic did not carry enough lifeboats for everyone on board – now the law makes sure all ships do

Lenin was a Russian icebreaker and the first surface ship to be driven by nuclear power

Nuclear power at sea

Only a small number of nuclear-powered civilian (non-military) ships have been built. The Soviet Union (now Russia) chose nuclear power for their large ice-breaking ships because it allows them to clear ice from the sea lanes off their northern coasts without having to keep returning to base to refuel.

Three nuclear reactors gave *Lenin* a maximum speed of 18 knots

Lenin could clear a 30-metre wide channel through pack ice 2.4 metres thick

Modern Ships

Most modern ships are built of steel and powered by diesel engines. They are usually equipped with a lot of automated machinery so that only a small crew is needed, as running ships cheaply is now typically more important than travelling at high speed. Water resistance slows a ship down, so a streamlined shape allows a ship to go faster. Satellites and computers control navigation, backed up by traditional instruments such as the sextant.

Specialist ships, such as express ferries, that need to travel more quickly commonly use twin-hull designs. Their narrow, smooth shapes cut more easily through the water. In the future, there will be more ships with two or three small, streamlined hulls, as they use less fuel to travel at higher speeds.

Luxury cruise ship

Ocean liners no longer carry passengers travelling from one port to another. Today, people have their holidays on board cruise ships. Instead of high speed, comfort has become the priority, so the ships have smooth-running diesel engines, stabilisers to help keep the ship steady, and full air conditioning.

Why do ships float?

The metal hull of a ship encloses a vast amount of air. This means a cubic metre of ship weighs much less than a cubic metre of water, so a ship can float. If the hull was solid metal the ship would sink very quickly.

The funnel, or stack, houses exhausts and air intakes for the main engines

Satellite communications equipment provides continuous contact with the mainland

Most cruise liners have many indoor and outdoor swimming pools

Shopping malls, cinemas, casinos and hairdressers are available on board

Passengers relax on the aft (rear) deck

Ropes can be used to help the ship dock

Some ships use rudders like this to steer; others have propellers mounted in steerable pods

Lifeboats and rafts are carried so passengers can escape in an emergency

Stabilisers

Most passenger ships use stabilisers to reduce roll (*see left*). These are often in the form of fins, like small wings. They use gyroscopes, computer software and hydraulic jacks to react quickly to the ship's roll and provide lift or downforce so the ship is kept level. When the sea is calm, they are retracted to prevent damage.

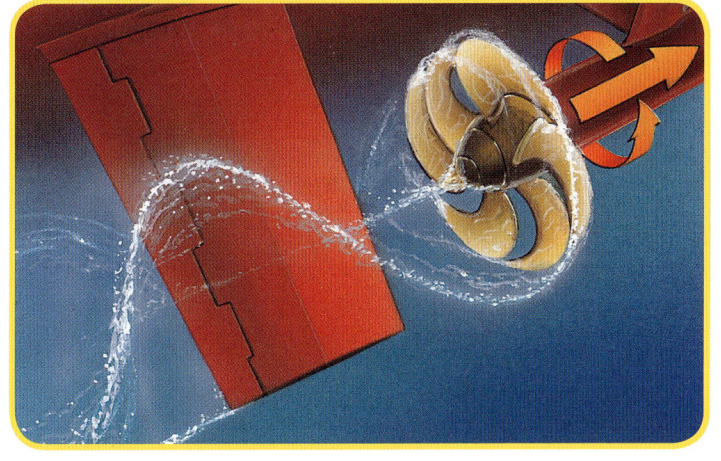

Propeller design

Great care goes into the design and manufacture of propellers. If just one blade is out of balance the smooth propulsion of a ship can be affected. Modern designs use several curved blades, and on some ships the blades can be angled to provide reverse thrust.

- Navigation, radio and radar equipment is carried on the main mast
- The most expensive cabins are higher up
- The bridge houses the ship's main controls
- The forward auditorium is a full-size theatre
- The forward weather deck can withstand heavy waves
- A bow thruster helps the ship to turn
- Stabiliser fins ensure a comfortable cruise
- Heavy equipment, fuel and stores are kept in the lowest part of the ship to aid stability
- Electric motors turn the propeller shafts
- Powerful diesel engines drive generators to provide electricity for all the ship's needs

Satellite navigation

Global Positioning System (GPS) satellites carry highly accurate atomic clocks and send time and position data to GPS receivers fitted to ships and aircraft. The receiver compares signals from two or more satellites to calculate its position to within a few metres. Buoys fitted with radio beacons also help to confirm a ship's position.

Fishing

Across the world there is high demand for fish and squid for food, so there are always large fleets of fishing vessels at sea. Because the demand for fish is so high, nations are able to monitor and control fishing up to 200 nautical miles from their coasts. Governments use aircraft or satellites to watch out for illegal fishing and protect their fish stocks. Inspectors can go aboard fishing vessels to check that regulations are being followed.

A fishing crew lives and works aboard ship 24 hours a day and is often paid according to the value of the catch. Even today, deep-sea fishing remains a physically dangerous job.

The crew can harness themselves to rails (I) so that they are not swept overboard in rough seas. Cranes (2) are used to handle the cables and nets.

Factory ship

Fishing grounds can be a long way from the country where the fish will be eaten. Some ships are equipped like factories so they can turn fish into products that can be sold at the end of the voyage, perhaps several months' journey away. The fish are gutted on board and the good quality fish fillets are sorted and deep frozen. The organs are stored or processed into fish oils and chemicals, and the offcuts, heads and bones turned into fishmeal, pastes and cheaper food products. Nothing is wasted, and the ship will stay at sea until the hold is full or fuel runs low.

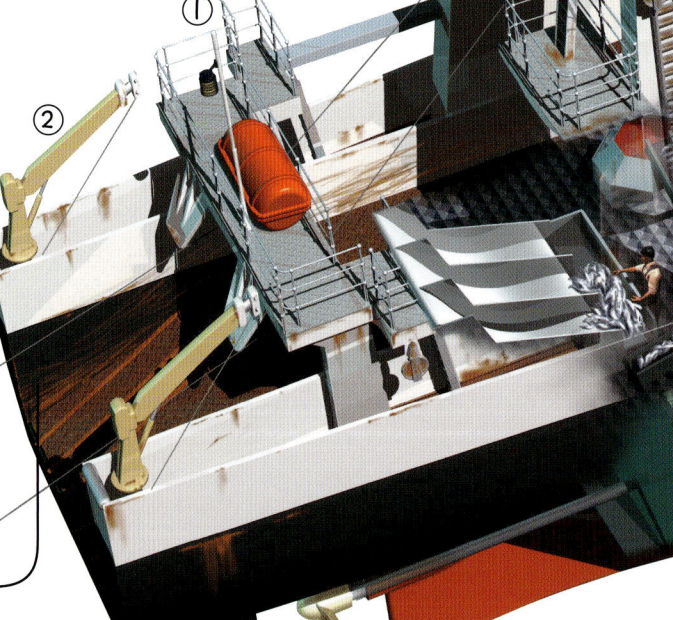

The A-frame holds the net and cables clear of obstructions on the stern

Winches (reels) are computer controlled to keep the net at the right depth

As the catch arrives, the crew set to work – gutting and processing the fish

The net is hauled back on board up the sloping stern ramp

A powerful propeller and double-hinged rudder make the ship easier to manoeuvre

The main diesel engine is heavy and sits low in the hull, helping stability

The engine room provides power for winches and the ship's electrical supply

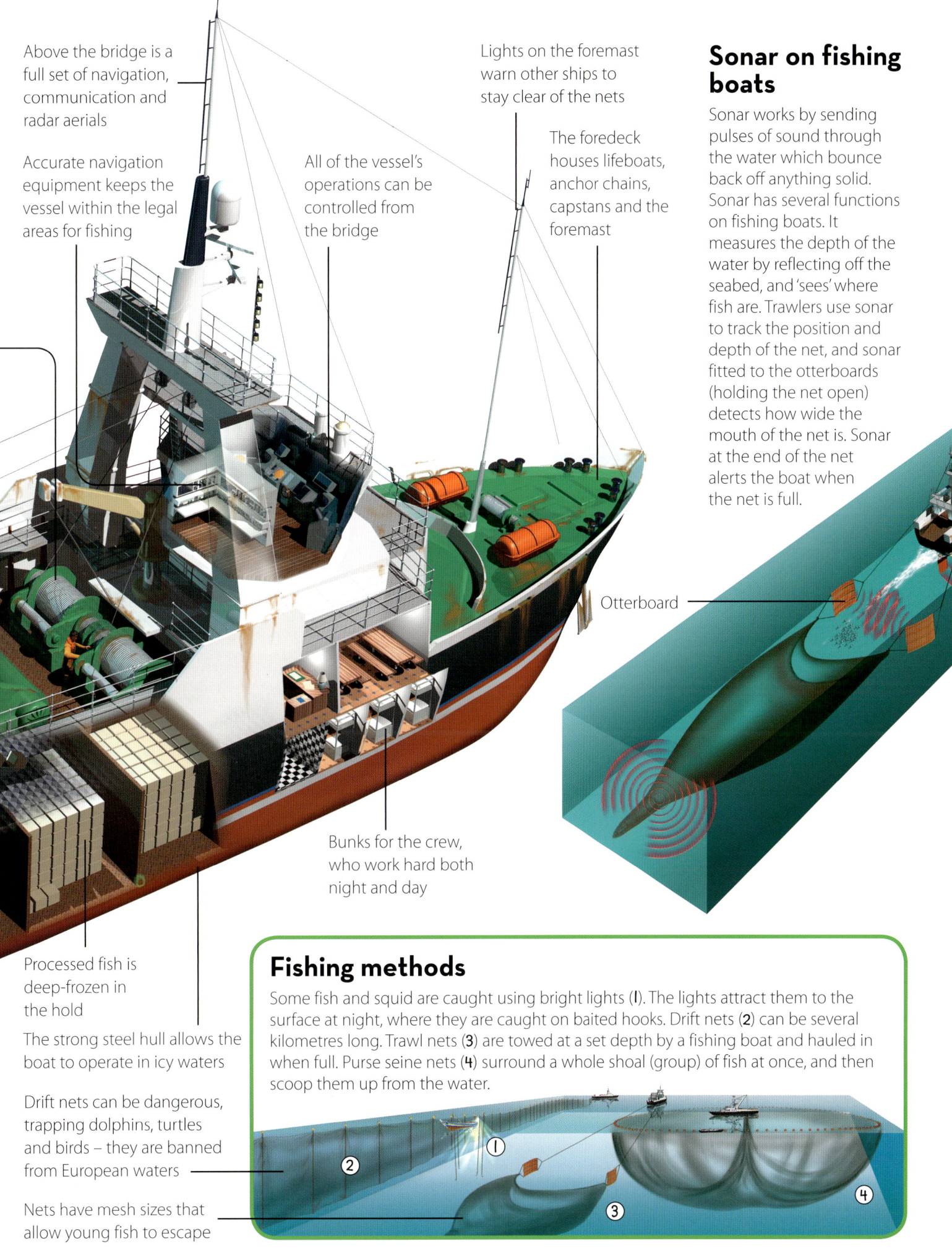

Above the bridge is a full set of navigation, communication and radar aerials

Accurate navigation equipment keeps the vessel within the legal areas for fishing

All of the vessel's operations can be controlled from the bridge

Lights on the foremast warn other ships to stay clear of the nets

The foredeck houses lifeboats, anchor chains, capstans and the foremast

Sonar on fishing boats

Sonar works by sending pulses of sound through the water which bounce back off anything solid. Sonar has several functions on fishing boats. It measures the depth of the water by reflecting off the seabed, and 'sees' where fish are. Trawlers use sonar to track the position and depth of the net, and sonar fitted to the otterboards (holding the net open) detects how wide the mouth of the net is. Sonar at the end of the net alerts the boat when the net is full.

Otterboard

Bunks for the crew, who work hard both night and day

Processed fish is deep-frozen in the hold

The strong steel hull allows the boat to operate in icy waters

Drift nets can be dangerous, trapping dolphins, turtles and birds – they are banned from European waters

Nets have mesh sizes that allow young fish to escape

Fishing methods

Some fish and squid are caught using bright lights (**1**). The lights attract them to the surface at night, where they are caught on baited hooks. Drift nets (**2**) can be several kilometres long. Trawl nets (**3**) are towed at a set depth by a fishing boat and hauled in when full. Purse seine nets (**4**) surround a whole shoal (group) of fish at once, and then scoop them up from the water.

Submarines

There are many submarines operating in the world's oceans. A few are small, carrying just two or three people. They are used for scientific research or construction work and stay underwater for only a few hours at a time.

Military submarines are much larger. There are two basic types: nuclear-powered missile-carrying submarines (*right*) and hunter-killers, which can be nuclear- or diesel-electric powered. The main reason why missiles are carried by submarines is that submarines are hidden underwater, which makes them harder for an enemy to find. However, the hunter-killer submarine is designed to find and destroy enemy missile-carrying submarines as well as an enemy's own hunter-killer submarines. Diesel-electric submarines are the quietest, so they are used for missions where stealth is important.

Staying hidden

The most important thing for military submarines is to avoid being detected, so they rarely surface, raise periscopes or use their radio to communicate with their base. Because sound carries far underwater, submarines are built to be as quiet as possible. Mechanics are taught to be careful not to drop their tools, and if necessary the submarine will sit motionless for days. It is impossible to be completely silent, though, and enemy hunter-killer submarines will listen out for the slightest hint that there might be a target nearby.

Ballistic missile submarine

Some countries use massive ballistic missile submarines that carry nuclear weapons. The submarines remain deep underwater or under ice caps for several months at a time. They are used as a 'deterrent': if a country were ever attacked with nuclear weapons, its submarines would launch a counterattack on the enemy country. The belief is that if an enemy country knows this threat of retaliation exists, it will be deterred (put off) from launching an attack in the first place.

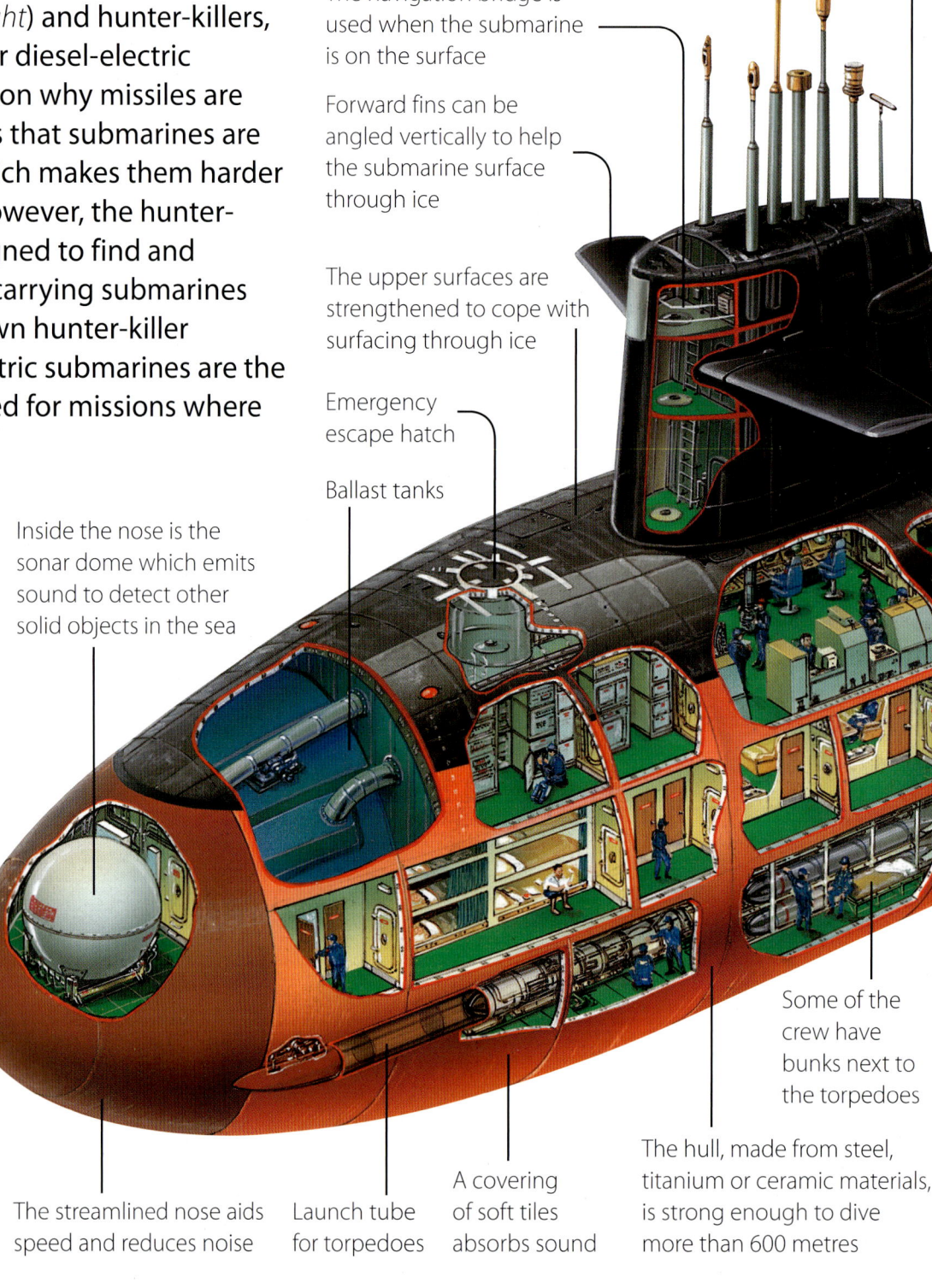

The navigation bridge is used when the submarine is on the surface

Forward fins can be angled vertically to help the submarine surface through ice

The upper surfaces are strengthened to cope with surfacing through ice

Emergency escape hatch

Ballast tanks

Inside the nose is the sonar dome which emits sound to detect other solid objects in the sea

The streamlined nose aids speed and reduces noise

Launch tube for torpedoes

A covering of soft tiles absorbs sound

Some of the crew have bunks next to the torpedoes

The hull, made from steel, titanium or ceramic materials, is strong enough to dive more than 600 metres

Detection by sound

A submarine uses sonar (sound navigation and ranging) to detect solid objects. Sonar can be active, where the submarine emits sounds which are reflected back from the target, or passive, where the submarine just monitors the sounds that other vessels or large animals are making.

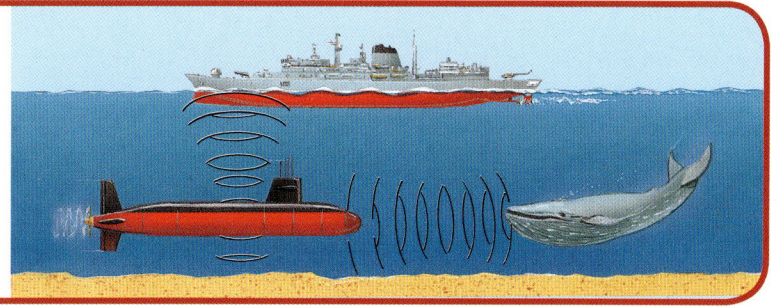

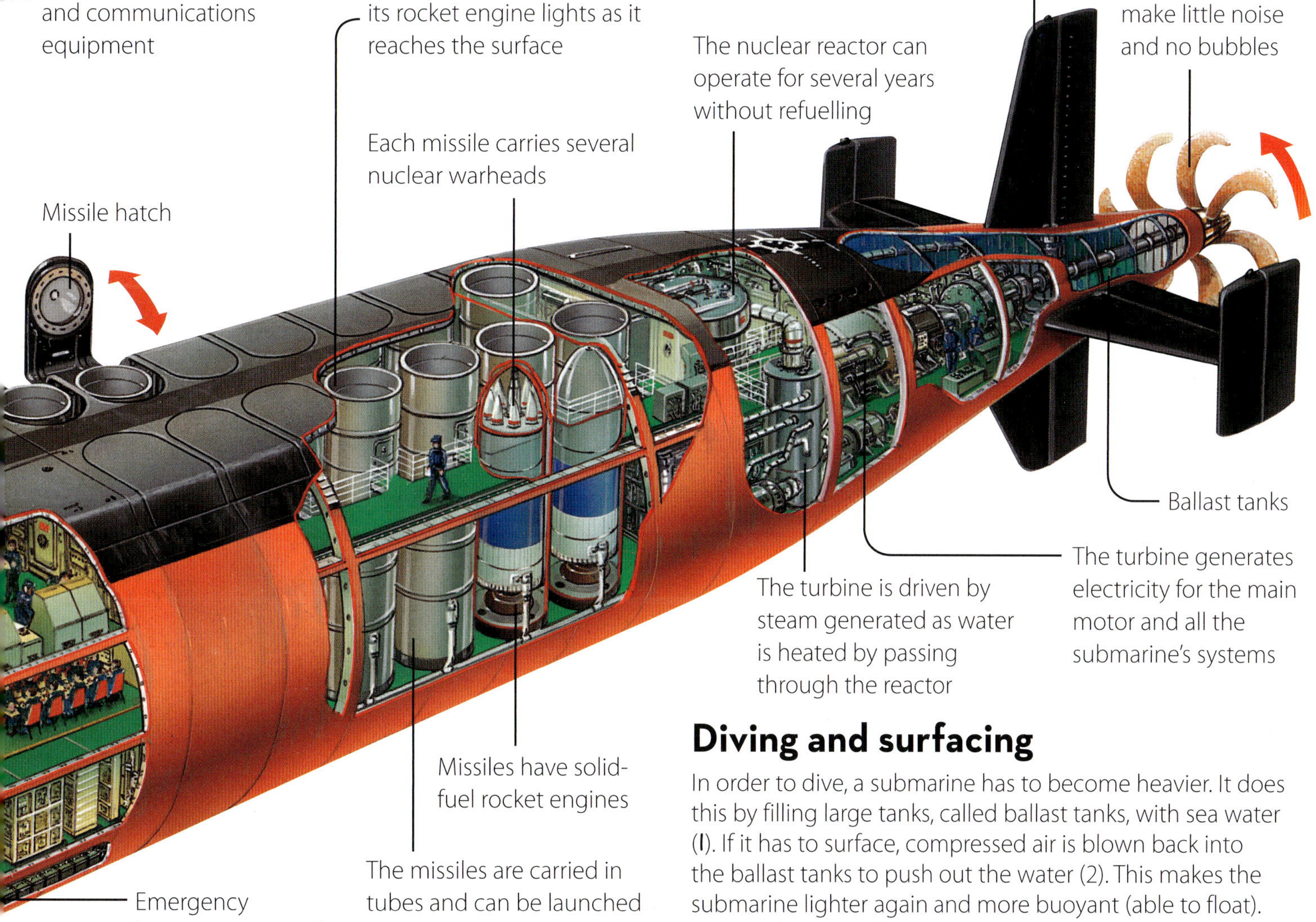

This tower carries the radar, periscopes and communications equipment

The missile is launched from the tube with a puff of gas – its rocket engine lights as it reaches the surface

Large rudders keep the submarine steady

The propeller is designed to make little noise and no bubbles

Missile hatch

Each missile carries several nuclear warheads

The nuclear reactor can operate for several years without refuelling

Ballast tanks

The turbine generates electricity for the main motor and all the submarine's systems

The turbine is driven by steam generated as water is heated by passing through the reactor

Missiles have solid-fuel rocket engines

The missiles are carried in tubes and can be launched while the submarine is underwater

Emergency batteries in case of main power failure

Diving and surfacing

In order to dive, a submarine has to become heavier. It does this by filling large tanks, called ballast tanks, with sea water (1). If it has to surface, compressed air is blown back into the ballast tanks to push out the water (2). This makes the submarine lighter again and more buoyant (able to float). Some submarines have been lost at sea when something has gone wrong with the ballast tank system.

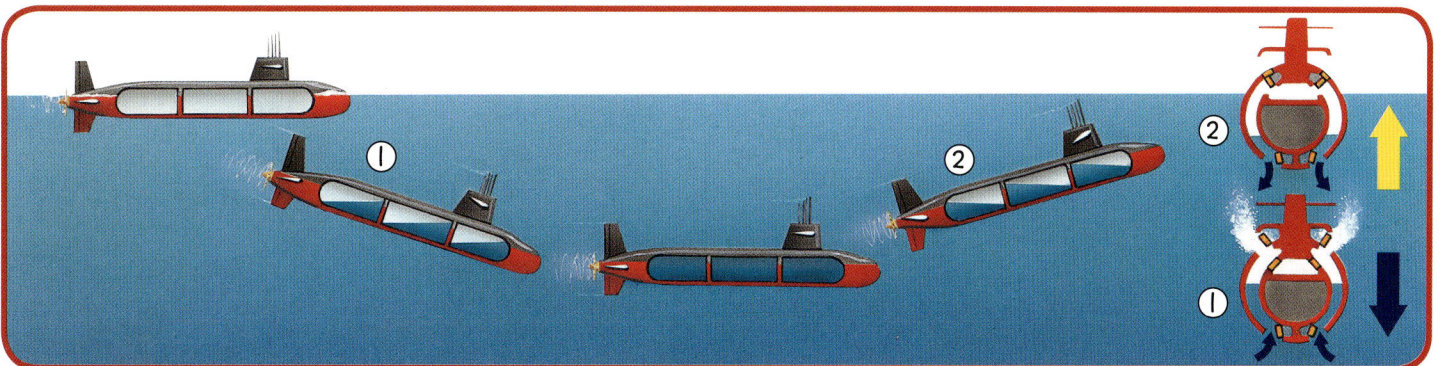

Scuba Diving

Scuba (Self-Contained Underwater Breathing Apparatus) enables people to explore underwater to a depth of around 30 metres, and sometimes even deeper. Below 60 metres, divers must use a special air mixture. Water pressure increases with depth and below 40 metres it has dangerous effects on a diver.

Pioneers like Jacques Cousteau and Hans Hass made scuba diving very popular, and today people dive all over the world. In fact, diving is so popular that it has become a problem in some places because if there are too many divers they can damage fragile coral reefs and affect the normal behaviour of fish.

Although diving is quite safe, training is essential. Divers learn safety drills and calculate how long they have been deep underwater so that they can return to the surface without getting the bends, a dangerous condition where air bubbles form inside the body.

Breathing apparatus

The tank strapped to the diver's back contains air for the diver to breathe. At the top of the air tank, level with the diver's lungs, is a valve called a regulator. Air passes through the regulator down a tube to the mouthpiece. The regulator reduces the pressure of the air that comes out of the tank.

The pressure is further reduced by the demand valve in the mouthpiece. This ensures that the air breathed is at the same pressure as that of the water around. Divers must breathe continuously and not hold their breath, as when they come up to the surface the reduced water pressure means air in their lungs expands and can cause the lungs to burst.

The air tank carries highly compressed (squashed) air mixtures

The face mask enables the diver to see underwater

Flash unit for camera

Electrical equipment must be waterproof

Air tube to the buoyancy compensator

Flow of exhaust air when breathing out

Underwater photography is popular with many sports divers

Demand valve

Diver breathes through valve

A diaphragm in the valve equalises the air and water pressure

The regulator controls the flow of air from the air tank and reduces the air's pressure

Pipe to the mouthpiece

Divers must take care not to damage coral with their fins

Swim fins help a diver to propel themselves through the water

The wetsuit's bright colours make the diver easier to spot underwater

Divers wear a knife to use if they get tangled up in nets, lines or seaweed

A buoyancy compensator (BC) is a jacket that can be inflated with air to help the diver rise to the surface

A weight belt allows the diver to sink easily

Neoprene wetsuit, hat, gloves and socks keep the diver warm

A compass is essential in murky waters

Many divers use a dive computer to keep track of time and calculate the speed at which they are rising to the surface

Compass and gauges show depth and amount of air left in tank

Wetsuits

Divers wear wetsuits made of neoprene foam rubber to insulate against the cold. Wetsuits are available in various thicknesses to suit different water temperatures. They are designed so that water leaks in through the neck, leg and arm holes. The diver's body heat then warms the thin layer of water between wetsuit and skin, keeping the diver warm for hours.

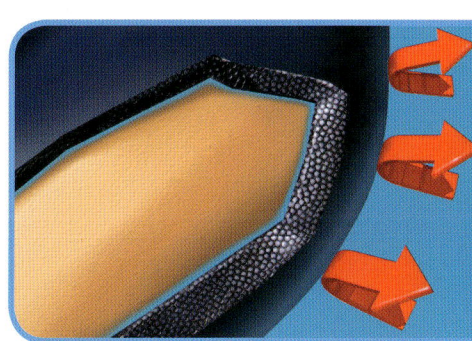

Hand signals

"OK" – everything is all right (on the surface)

"Not OK' – help needed (on the surface)

"Are you OK?" or "I am OK"

"I'm out of air!"

Though there are gadgets that enable divers to speak underwater, most divers don't have them, so they rely on hand signals. There is an international code of hand signals so that divers can dive safely anywhere in the world. Divers never dive alone. They always have a fellow diver to keep an eye on them and watch out for distress signals.

Submersibles

Submersibles are small, deep-diving vehicles that were first used to search for sunken wreckage of lost aircraft, ships and weapons. Today, they are most often used by scientists to explore features of the deep ocean floor, such as trenches and volcanic ridges. Compared with military submarines, submersibles cannot stay underwater for very long – usually a few hours, or a day or two at the most. However, they are more useful for scientific studies as they can dive far deeper, some to 6,000 metres or more. They also have windows, camera systems and mechanical 'hands' so that the crew can view and handle things at the bottom of the ocean.

Today, rigid diving suits can almost do the same job as submersibles and some, such as the Newtsuit, can use propellers mounted on a backpack to move about.

Trieste

Trieste was designed to reach the greatest depths possible. On 23 January 1960 she carried Jacques Piccard and Don Walsh to a record depth of 10,912 metres at the bottom of a gorge in the Pacific Ocean called Challenger Deep. Its record remained unbroken until DSV *Limiting Factor* reached a depth of 10,928 metres in 2019. *Trieste* had two ballast tanks filled with heavy iron weights. To surface, the weights were released, making *Trieste* lighter and able to rise. A tank filled with petrol gave buoyancy. The crew sat inside a steel sphere, called a gondola.

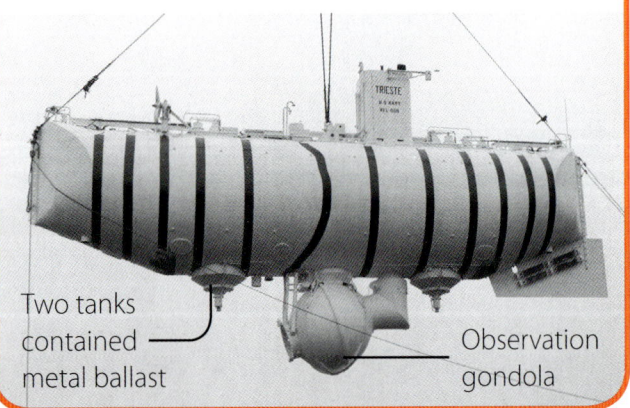

Two tanks contained metal ballast

Observation gondola

- Underwater telephone transmitter
- The tower is brightly coloured so *Alvin* can be easily spotted on the surface
- The sonar scanner can spot hidden obstacles
- Video cameras record everything happening outside. Powerful lights penetrate the darkness
- The cabin for the crew is a metal sphere
- Mechanical arms collect objects from the ocean floor
- With the help of laser technology, arm control is precise
- The collecting cage can carry sample bottles, rock specimens and items from shipwrecks

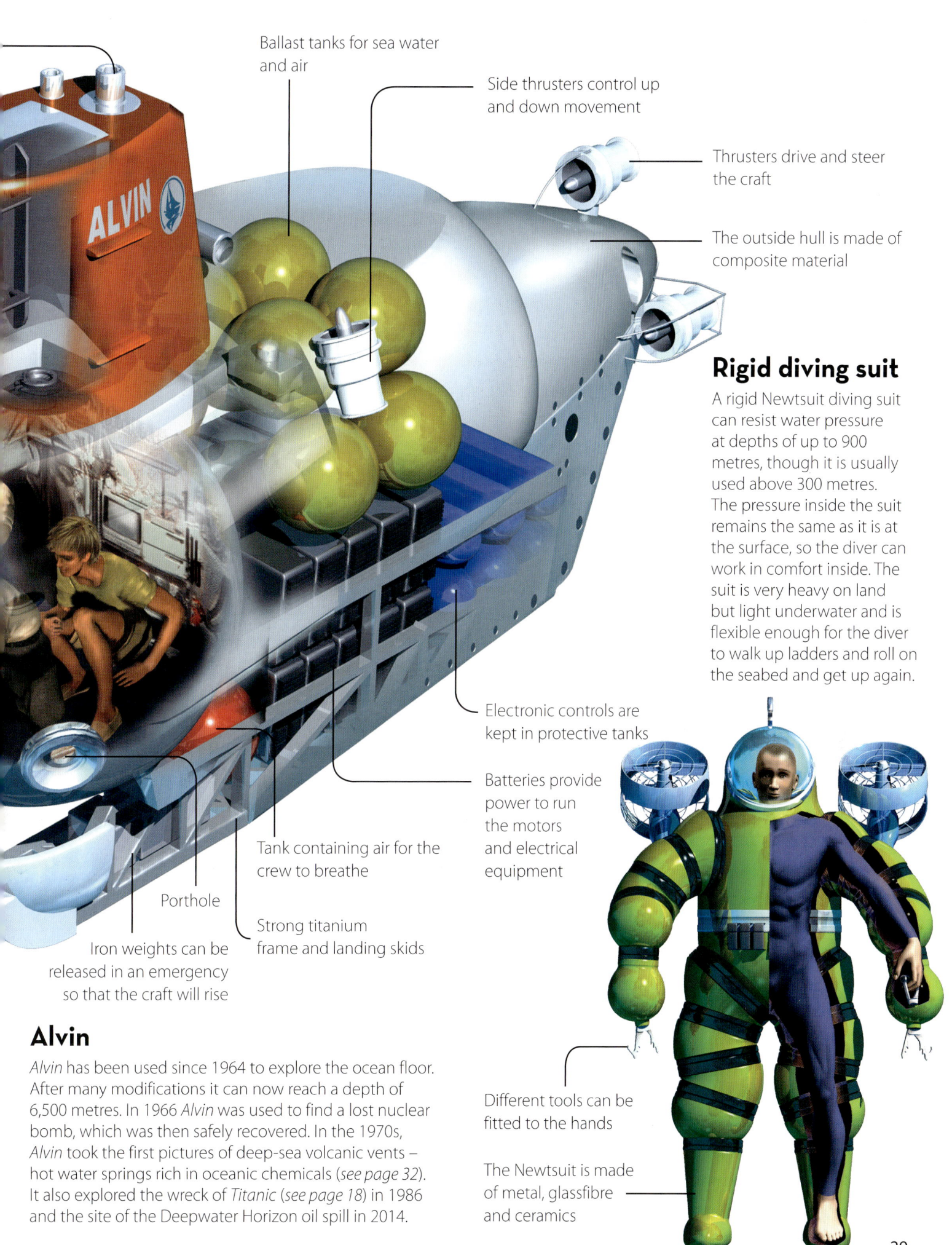

Ballast tanks for sea water and air

Side thrusters control up and down movement

Thrusters drive and steer the craft

The outside hull is made of composite material

Electronic controls are kept in protective tanks

Batteries provide power to run the motors and electrical equipment

Tank containing air for the crew to breathe

Porthole

Strong titanium frame and landing skids

Iron weights can be released in an emergency so that the craft will rise

Alvin

Alvin has been used since 1964 to explore the ocean floor. After many modifications it can now reach a depth of 6,500 metres. In 1966 *Alvin* was used to find a lost nuclear bomb, which was then safely recovered. In the 1970s, *Alvin* took the first pictures of deep-sea volcanic vents – hot water springs rich in oceanic chemicals (*see page 32*). It also explored the wreck of *Titanic* (*see page 18*) in 1986 and the site of the Deepwater Horizon oil spill in 2014.

Rigid diving suit

A rigid Newtsuit diving suit can resist water pressure at depths of up to 900 metres, though it is usually used above 300 metres. The pressure inside the suit remains the same as it is at the surface, so the diver can work in comfort inside. The suit is very heavy on land but light underwater and is flexible enough for the diver to walk up ladders and roll on the seabed and get up again.

Different tools can be fitted to the hands

The Newtsuit is made of metal, glassfibre and ceramics

Shipwrecks

In an average year around 100 ships sink because of accidents, severe storms and, most commonly, human error. Some of these wrecks cause major pollution problems, but the ocean's natural processes are able to cope with many types of waste. Iron-eating bacteria start working on the hull, worms feed on the wood and chemical action sorts out what is left. After a few hundred years, a lot of the shipwreck will have gone, leaving behind few clues for explorers.

As underwater technology has advanced, getting valuable items from shipwrecks has become easier. At first, only recovering treasure and cannons was considered worth the risk involved. Later, it became possible to raise whole wrecks in one piece by patching up holes and pumping in air.

The development of deep-ocean exploration systems was driven by the need to find missing submarines and nuclear weapons during the Cold War years. It has resulted in spectacular finds, including Dr Robert Ballard's discovery of the wrecks of *Titanic* and the World War II German battleship, *Bismarck*.

Wreck hunting

Finding deep wrecks is not easy because the oceans are so large. First there is a survey of the area where the wreck might be, using side-scan sonar and cameras mounted on sleds. When the wreck is found, detailed exploration can begin using video cameras attached to remotely operated vehicles (ROVs). A submersible like *Alvin* may be used so the explorers can examine the wreck more closely.

Side-scan sonar

A side-scan sonar (*right*) gives a one-colour image of shadows. Computers process the data to improve the picture quality but recognising what the image shows still requires skill and experience.

Viewing the remains

An ROV camera travels around and inside the wreck (*below*), capturing images of objects it finds. Any bodies would have decomposed or been eaten by sea creatures long ago.

The crew work in a titanium sphere with thick windows – water pressure at 3,000 metres is 300 times greater than atmospheric pressure

The submersible's propeller is protected by a light covering so that pieces of rigging, wire, or rope will not trap the vessel

A remote manipulator arm lifts items from the ocean floor – some pieces may be brought to the surface for closer examination

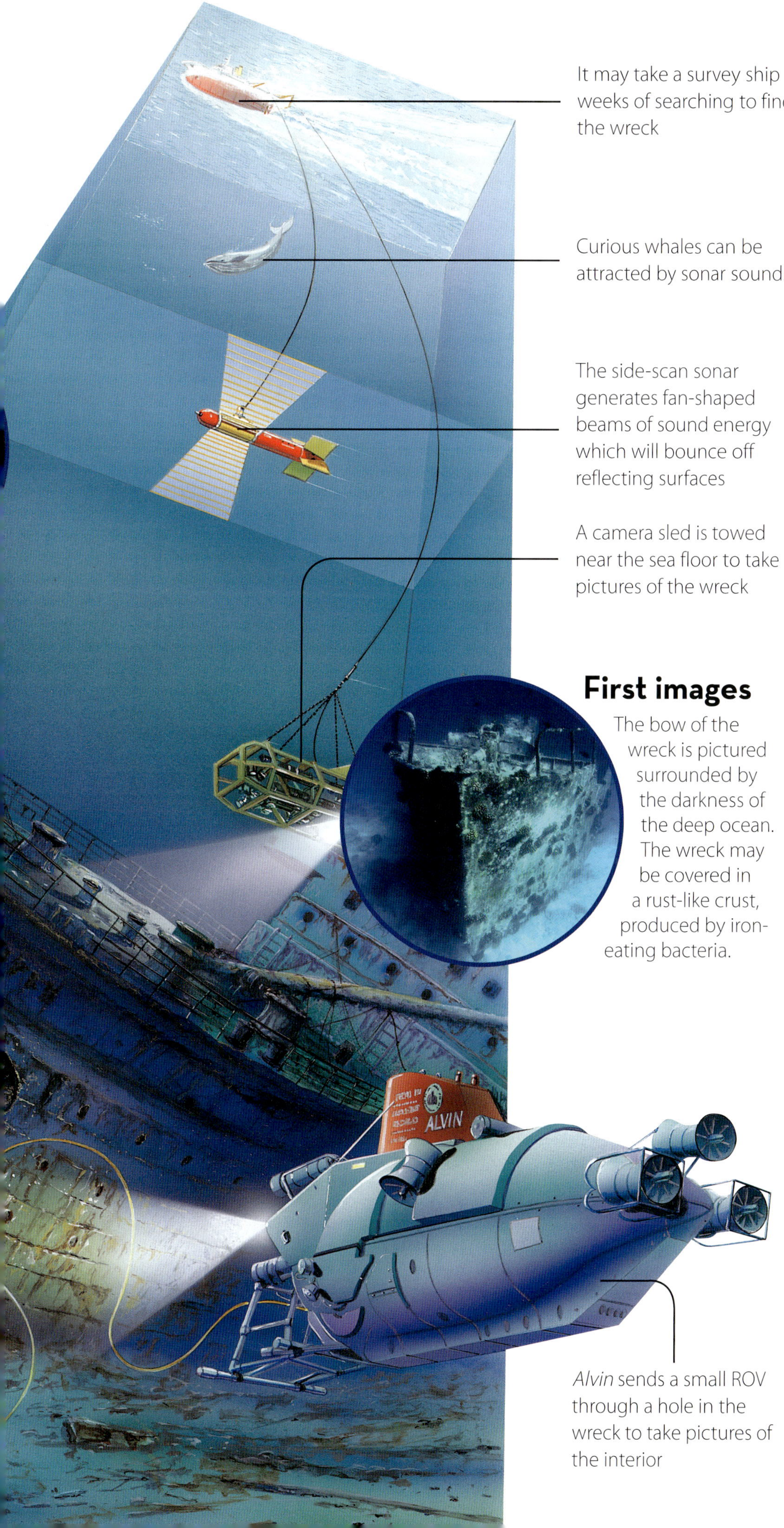

It may take a survey ship weeks of searching to find the wreck

Curious whales can be attracted by sonar sounds

The side-scan sonar generates fan-shaped beams of sound energy which will bounce off reflecting surfaces

A camera sled is towed near the sea floor to take pictures of the wreck

First images

The bow of the wreck is pictured surrounded by the darkness of the deep ocean. The wreck may be covered in a rust-like crust, produced by iron-eating bacteria.

Alvin sends a small ROV through a hole in the wreck to take pictures of the interior

Looking for ancient wrecks

In the warm, clear waters of the Mediterranean, marine archaeologists hunt for the wrecks of ancient Greek, Roman and Persian ships. The wooden parts will have been eaten away unless they were well buried, but metal and ceramic remains can be found by a submersible detector.

A diver photographs the cargo of a Roman shipwreck. A survey grid (*below*) enables the position of items to be accurately recorded.

A cannon is raised using lifting bags that are filled with air at the sea-bed (*below*). The diver releases air pressure to control ascent speed. Larger bags can raise aircraft, ships and submarines.

Ocean Life

The oceans teem with a wide variety of life, from tiny bacteria to huge whales. Scientists believe that life on Earth first began in the oceans. Today, land animals still have salty blood – perhaps this is a sign of their ancient connection to the oceans.

Life exists throughout the ocean, even on the ocean floor in the deepest, darkest trenches and in icy polar waters. At the surface, phytoplankton (tiny floating plants) use the Sun's energy to make food. Animals feed on the plankton and are in turn eaten by larger hunters and scavengers. In very deep water where there is no light for plants to grow, and in the thick mud of the ocean floor, worms, bacteria and other creatures feed on organic material that has sunk all the way down from the waters above.

There is one very unusual group of creatures on the ocean floor which feed on chemicals rather than animal or plant matter. They live near hot water springs.

Something for everyone

In the ocean, every possible niche, or living space, is used by one or more life forms. New creatures are still being discovered as researchers learn more about the deep oceans.

Scientists were amazed to discover that life could exist around deep-sea hot water vents. Water gushes up from these volcanic vents at temperatures of 400 °C carrying a strong mixture of dissolved chemicals.

The source of energy for most animals stems from the Sun: animals eat plants which use sunlight to make their food energy. But the creatures living near the volcanic vents get their energy from eating bacteria which change the chemicals they have absorbed into energy.

In warm, sunlit waters, plants and animals thrive

Most of the drifting 'plankton' is made up of phytoplankton (tiny plants) and zooplankton (tiny animals), including larvae (young forms of animals)

The Portuguese man o' war catches its prey with long, venomous tentacles

The dim twilight zone (down to 1,000 metres) is home to many fish, like these hatchet fish

Few animals live in the dark, cold bathypelagic zone (down to 4,000 metres)

Tripod fish and sea cucumber

Minerals from the hot water form chimneys around the vents

Giant tube worms grow up to 3 metres long

Deep-sea crabs and fish thrive near a hot water vent

Sunlight provides the energy that starts the food chain

Small fish eat plankton

Food chains

In the open ocean, phytoplankton are eaten by zooplankton, which in turn are eaten by small fish. The small fish are eaten by larger fish and squid, which are eaten by toothed whales and sharks. This is called a food chain. Each group of animals is an important link in the chain as food for another group.

All the oceans' plants and many of their animals live in the sunlit zone (down to 200 metres)

Squid eat small fish

Sperm whales eat squid

Sharks have existed for millions of years

Octopuses are intelligent creatures found in both deep and shallow water

Gulper eels can dislocate their jaws to swallow large prey

Brittle stars are able to live at great depths

Angler fish attract prey with a light-emitting 'lantern' above their head

The abyssal zone is dark and very cold

Gill arches

How fish breathe

Fish do not have lungs, but breathe using similar organs called gills, which can extract the oxygen dissolved in sea water. The fish gulps water into its mouth, then pushes it out between the gill arches, which are lined with blood-filled cells. Here, oxygen passes from the sea water into the fish's blood, and waste gases flow out of the fish into the sea water. Some of the gas which the fish extracts from the water inflates a swim bladder, which helps to stop the fish from sinking.

33

Coastal Life

Animals and plants that live on the coast need to be hardy and adaptable as they have to cope with periods in and out of the water as the sea level rises and falls with the tide. Some seaweeds produce slime to help stop them from drying out at low tide. Many animals burrow into the wet sand, hide under seaweed or close their shells while the tide is out. Coastal plants and animals in exposed places also need to be strong enough to withstand the waves and be able to adapt to changes in the saltiness of the water when it rains.

A greater variety of animals and plants live in rockpools, where sea water remains after the tide goes out. They do not suffer from drying out, but they still have to cope with how rainwater affects the saltiness of the pool and changes in temperature as the pool warms up in the sun or cools down in the cold.

Coastal life zones

The splash zone lies above high tide but is regularly sprayed with salt water. It's a hard place to live and few species make their home here. Those that do are typically snails and yellow, orange and black lichens.

The intertidal zone, between high and low tide, is home to creatures such as barnacles, limpets, mussels, sea anemones and crabs. Plants include brown, green and red seaweed.

Many more kinds of plants and animals live below the low tide level. In colder waters, huge forests of large brown seaweed, called kelp, live on rocks, sheltering delicate red seaweed, fish and many other animals, while in warm waters, coral reefs thrive.

Sand, gravel, mud and rock form the seabed

The blades of this giant kelp stretch up towards the surface waters to receive sunlight

Seaweed clings firmly to rocks so that it is not swept out to sea

Burrowing on the beach

Many animals burrow in the sand on a beach. With her hind flippers, the female loggerhead turtle digs a hole in which to lay her eggs (1). Razor shells (2) are long and have a powerful 'foot' at the bottom that helps them move up or down. The sand gaper (3) has an oval shell and feeds through two tubes that stretch up to the surface. Sea potatoes (4) are burrowing sea urchins. The sea mouse (5) is actually a worm covered in fine hairs. Lugworms (6) swallow sand to feed, passing out what's left as a worm cast.

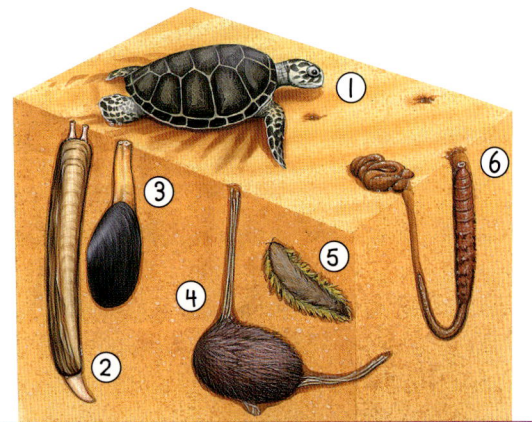

Seabirds often nest on cliffs near to their food supply

Lichens are formed by fungi and algae living together

Sea slaters feed on seaweed and dead animals

Periwinkles can be rolled by waves without being damaged

Limpets

When the tide goes out, limpets clamp their shells firmly to the rock to stop their bodies from drying out. A sucker-like foot allows them to move across rocks.

A cross-section of a limpet reveals its stomach and other organs

A crab's soft under-body is protected by the hard shell on its back

Air-filled sacs keep some kinds of seaweed afloat

Crabs

Several types of crab are found on the coast. Their soft bodies are protected by hard shells. They use their pincers to crush the shells of their prey.

Mangroves

Mangrove trees are unusual in that they can live in salty sea water. The mass of tangled roots of a mangrove swamp provide a home for young fish, saltwater crocodiles and sea snakes. The mudskipper (*above*) is a small fish that can climb out of the water and up the mangrove roots using its front fins. It feeds on small animals found in the mud at low tide.

At the centre of the sea urchin, above five sharp teeth, lies its stomach

Sea urchins and starfish

Sea urchins have a protective outer covering of spines and a shell made of layers of interlocking plates. The spines and sucker-like feet allow urchins to move around on the seabed and shore. Five teeth under the body scrape food off rocks.

Starfish belong to the same family of animals as sea urchins. Under the arms of a starfish are rows of tube-like feet that are used for moving and feeding.

Seabirds

Seabirds can be found in all of the world's oceans, from the freezing waters of the Antarctic to the warmth of tropical lagoons. Some, such as the albatross and storm petrel, spend most of their lives at sea, returning to the land only once a year to breed and moult (shed old feathers).

Seabirds eat fish, squid, or plankton and they may travel thousands of kilometres to find them. To stay warm in cold sea water most birds have a layer of fat under their skin and they produce a waxy substance that they rub onto their feathers to keep them waterproof. An exception is the cormorant, which has to rest out of the water with its wings outstretched to dry in the sun.

While seabirds have few natural enemies, many are killed accidentally by humans – by pollution or from becoming tangled in fishing nets.

The brown pelican

Brown pelicans live in coastal areas of the USA. They have a large baggy pouch on the underside of their beak which they use to catch lots of small fish to eat.

The pelican flies above the water looking for fish swimming near the surface. When it spots a shoal, the bird dives gracefully into the water, taking the fish by surprise. The pelican swims around, scooping the fish into its pouch, then returns to the surface to swallow them.

The brown pelican flies several metres above the surface looking for fish

When it spots a group of fish near the surface, it dives into the sea, folding back its wings

The storm petrel hovers just above the surface

Once in the water, the pelican scoops up as many fish as possible

The auk uses its stumpy wings to 'fly' underwater

Fish slide head first down the pelican's gullet, then pass into its stomach

Feeding

There are many ways to catch seafood. Skimmers fly low over the surface at night using the tip of their beak to scoop up small fish and shrimps. The storm petrel hovers over the sea surface, picking up individual fish. The auk, from the family that includes the puffin, guillemot and razorbill, dives into the water to chase fish using its powerful, stumpy wings and webbed feet. The albatross glides effortlessly, landing on the water occasionally to catch fish or squid.

The blue-footed booby has a shallow diving angle

Albatrosses catch fish while floating on the surface

Skimmers fly from dusk to dawn, scooping up food from the surface

The cormorant has a steep, streamlined dive and uses its feet to push itself through the water

Penguins catch fish and squid by swimming quickly underwater

Fish, squid and plankton are food for seabirds

Puffin nest

Puffins live in noisy groups on isolated islands away from land predators such as rats and foxes. They nest inside tunnels, amongst rocks or in abandoned rabbit burrows. Puffins can dig their own burrows using their sharp bills and feet.

Kittiwake nest

Kittiwakes attach their cup-shaped nests to narrow cliff-side ledges using their droppings as a kind of glue.

Guillemot nest

Guillemots nest on rock ledges, with a sheer drop to the sea below. They lay pointed eggs which are less likely to fall off if they are accidentally knocked.

Coral Reefs

Coral looks and feels like rock but is made by tiny animals related to jellyfish and sea anemones. These animals, called polyps, build a stony cup-shaped skeleton around them. As the polyps multiply, new polyps grow on the skeletons of dead polyps. Thousands of these polyps together form a clump of coral. Coral is highly sensitive to pollution and rapid changes in sea level and temperature. It mainly grows in clear, shallow, tropical waters.

Coral reefs form walls following coastlines, often with a calm, shallow lagoon inside. Life flourishes in these sheltered, food-rich lagoons. Thousands of brightly coloured fish make use of the coral reef in different ways, some grazing, others hiding from predators (creatures that hunt them for food).

More species of fish can be found on a reef (*above left*) than in any other ocean habitat, but pollution, rising ocean temperatures and tourism all threaten global coral reefs, causing many to die off (*above right*). Scientists can help some to recover, but these fragile ecosystems need protection if they are to survive.

Sea cucumbers are in the same animal group as starfish and sea urchins

Butterfly fish recognise each other by their markings

Giant clams grow slowly and may live for a hundred years

Delicate sea fans are found in deeper water away from damaging waves

Clownfish are able to hide among anemones, which sting other fish

The crown-of-thorns starfish attacks coral

A grouper lets a cleaner wrasse remove parasites living in its mouth

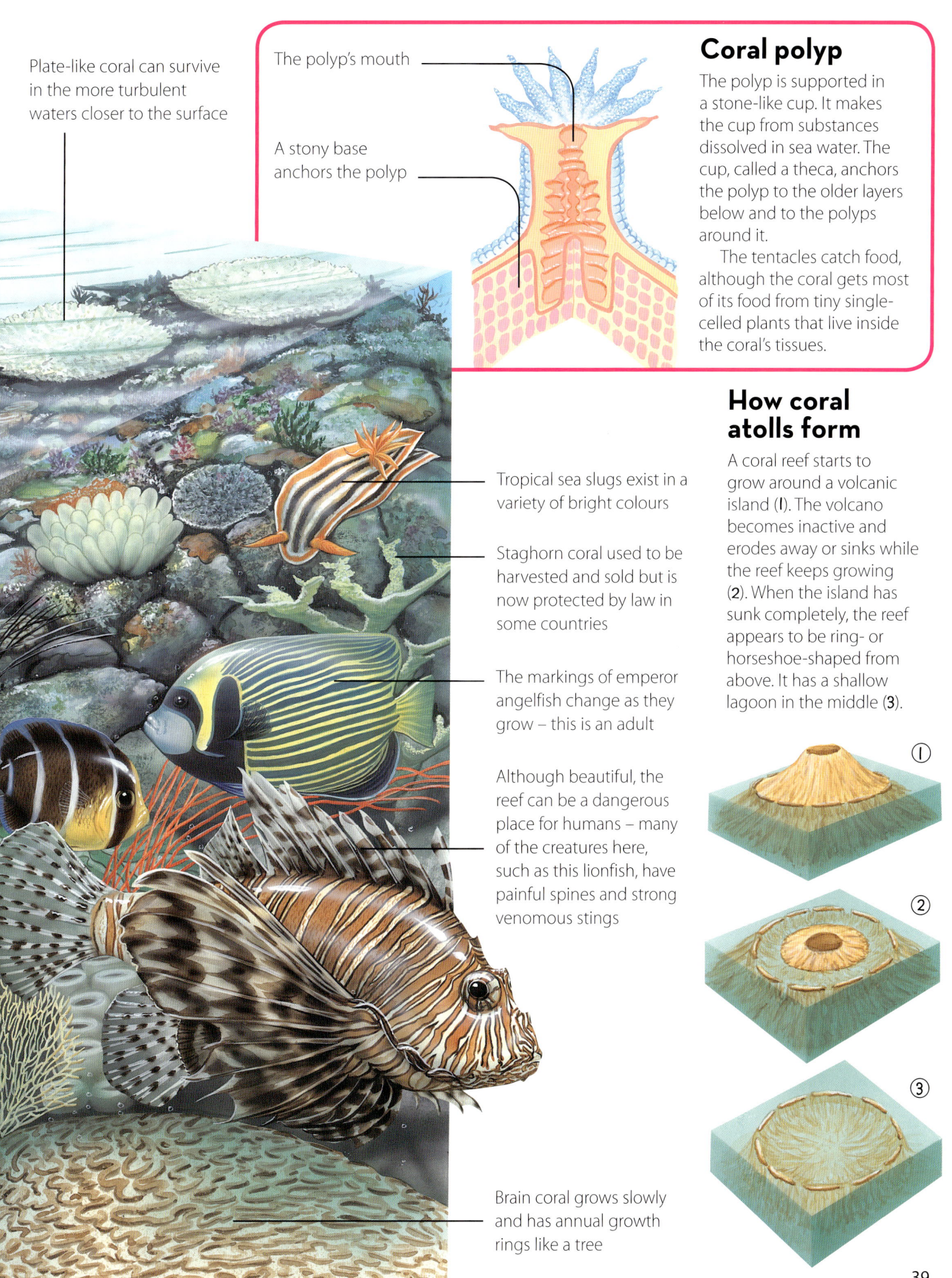

Plate-like coral can survive in the more turbulent waters closer to the surface

The polyp's mouth

A stony base anchors the polyp

Coral polyp

The polyp is supported in a stone-like cup. It makes the cup from substances dissolved in sea water. The cup, called a theca, anchors the polyp to the older layers below and to the polyps around it.

The tentacles catch food, although the coral gets most of its food from tiny single-celled plants that live inside the coral's tissues.

How coral atolls form

A coral reef starts to grow around a volcanic island (1). The volcano becomes inactive and erodes away or sinks while the reef keeps growing (2). When the island has sunk completely, the reef appears to be ring- or horseshoe-shaped from above. It has a shallow lagoon in the middle (3).

Tropical sea slugs exist in a variety of bright colours

Staghorn coral used to be harvested and sold but is now protected by law in some countries

The markings of emperor angelfish change as they grow – this is an adult

Although beautiful, the reef can be a dangerous place for humans – many of the creatures here, such as this lionfish, have painful spines and strong venomous stings

Brain coral grows slowly and has annual growth rings like a tree

39

Ocean Pollution

Almost all rivers and drainage systems eventually flow into the ocean, carrying waste products from human activities out to sea. The oceans have become an enormous sink for chemicals, sewage and rubbish as a result of wars, accidents and deliberate dumping. Of course, the oceans are very large and not all pollutants (polluting substances) cause major problems. Some bacteria can will eat up oil spills, or even digest steel, and over many years the oceans can clean themselves quite well. But if pollutants are concentrated, a great deal of damage can be done. Coastal waters beside large cities, intensively farmed land, or heavy industries can become so polluted that natural systems cannot cope. The result can be death for marine life, ugly pollution along coastlines and damage to the health of the human population. Many countries are trying hard to limit and control pollution.

Poisonous waters

There are so many sources of pollution that it is difficult to know exactly what is going into the sea. Chemicals that are harmless on their own get mixed with others and produce dangerous mixtures that can have unexpected effects, such as turning male fish into females. Nutrients (food) in sewage and fertilisers used on farms can cause poisonous plankton to grow at a rapid rate, causing harmful algal blooms.

Some of the chemicals sprayed on crops end up in rivers and oceans

Housing developments near the coast increase local pollution levels

Sewers can leak into groundwater and spoil water supplies

Poisonous plankton thrive in some polluted seas, colouring the water

Sewage sludge dumped from a ship is poisonous to marine life

Dumped mining waste can poison the water, smother the seabed and kill marine life

Fertiliser damage

Farms use large quantities of artificial fertiliser so that they can grow as many crops as possible. Some of the fertiliser gets washed into rivers by rainfall and carried into coastal waters where the local marine plants start growing at a greater rate. The fast-growing plants can choke the spaces where other animals and plants would normally live, and when the plants start to rot they begin to smell and attract many insects.

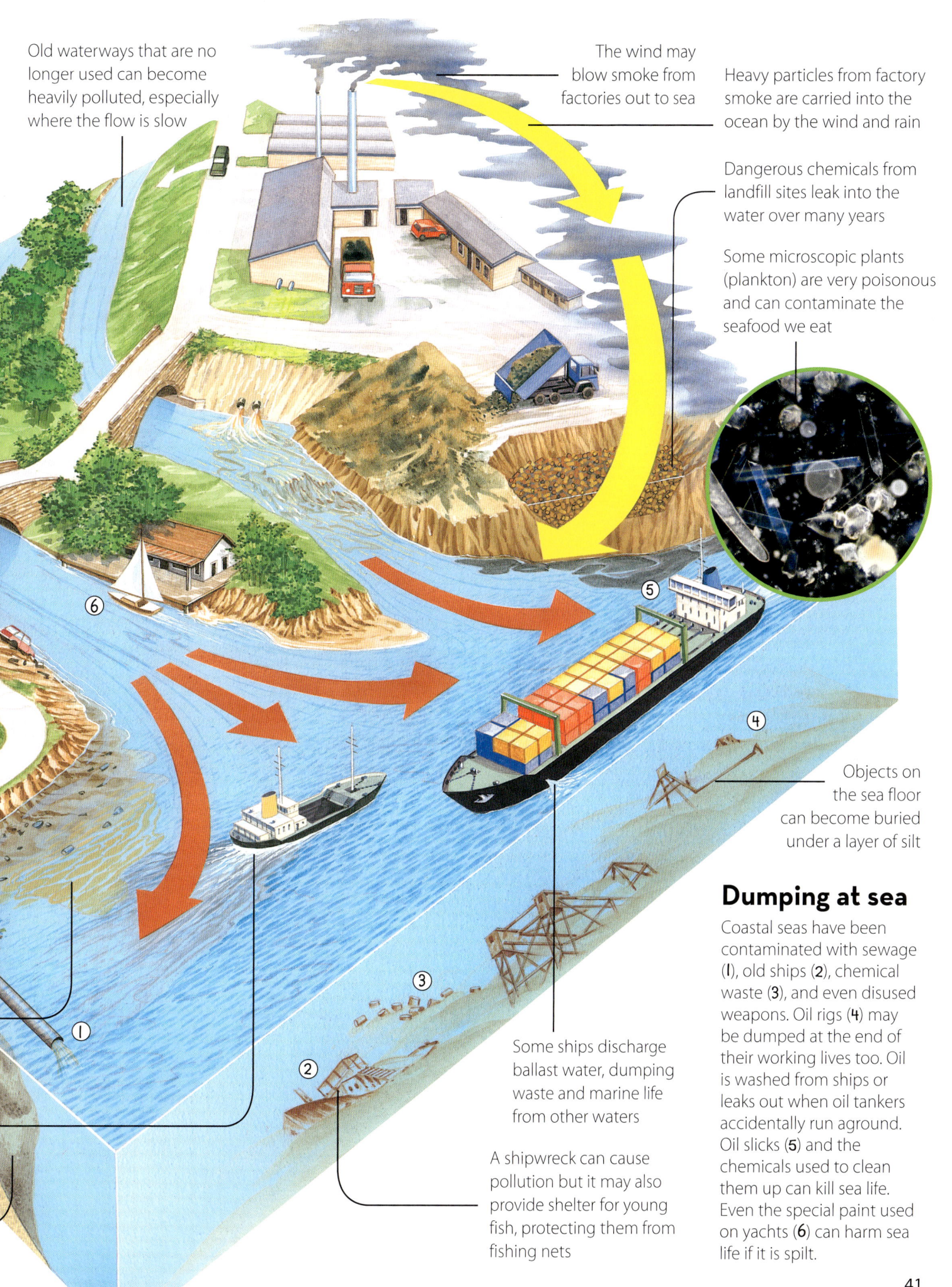

Old waterways that are no longer used can become heavily polluted, especially where the flow is slow

The wind may blow smoke from factories out to sea

Heavy particles from factory smoke are carried into the ocean by the wind and rain

Dangerous chemicals from landfill sites leak into the water over many years

Some microscopic plants (plankton) are very poisonous and can contaminate the seafood we eat

Objects on the sea floor can become buried under a layer of silt

Some ships discharge ballast water, dumping waste and marine life from other waters

A shipwreck can cause pollution but it may also provide shelter for young fish, protecting them from fishing nets

Dumping at sea

Coastal seas have been contaminated with sewage (1), old ships (2), chemical waste (3), and even disused weapons. Oil rigs (4) may be dumped at the end of their working lives too. Oil is washed from ships or leaks out when oil tankers accidentally run aground. Oil slicks (5) and the chemicals used to clean them up can kill sea life. Even the special paint used on yachts (6) can harm sea life if it is spilt.

Mining the Sea

Beneath the ocean floor there are vast reserves of oil, gas and coal, as well as other minerals and metals that are of value to humans. The ocean floor has valuable reserves of sand and gravel which can be used in road building and construction. Occasionally, the sand and gravel contains diamonds or other precious substances.

Where a resource is in plentiful supply on land, like coal, for example, there is not much point in mining it from the sea. The cost and difficulty of drilling exploration wells and building platforms out at sea is high, but oil and gas are so valuable that this is still thought to be worthwhile.

In the future, as reserves of raw materials run out on the land, other products may be mined from the sea.

Oil platform

The superstructure is built of several modules, which are lifted onto the steel framework, called a jacket, by cranes. There are modules for power, engineering, pump rooms, accommodation, catering, medical services and entertainment.

Flare stack burns off excess gas

⑤ A pipe from this derrick carries oil and gas to the surface

Gas turbine exhausts

The jacket (framework) is maintained by divers and underwater robots

Formation of oil and gas

Organic matter such as plankton drifts to the seabed and gets buried (*top right*). Over time, the layers of decomposing matter deepen, and their temperature and pressure increase. Chemical reactions and bacteria slowly change the organic matter into hydrocarbons such as oil and gas (*middle*). Along geological faults the oil and gas may become trapped beneath layers of rock (*bottom*).

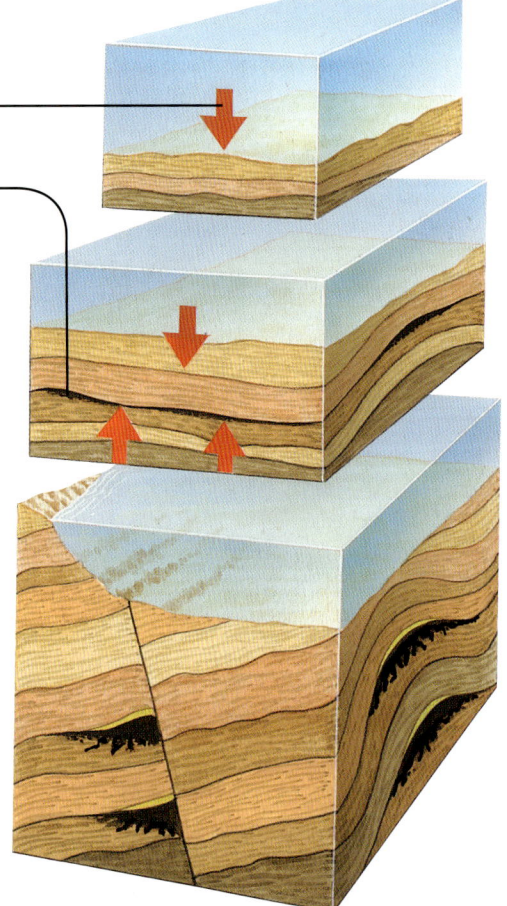

Continuous rain of organic material onto the seabed

Increasing pressure and temperature gradually cause hydrocarbons to form

Helicopters are used to transfer crew, supplies and equipment between the mainland and the drilling platform.

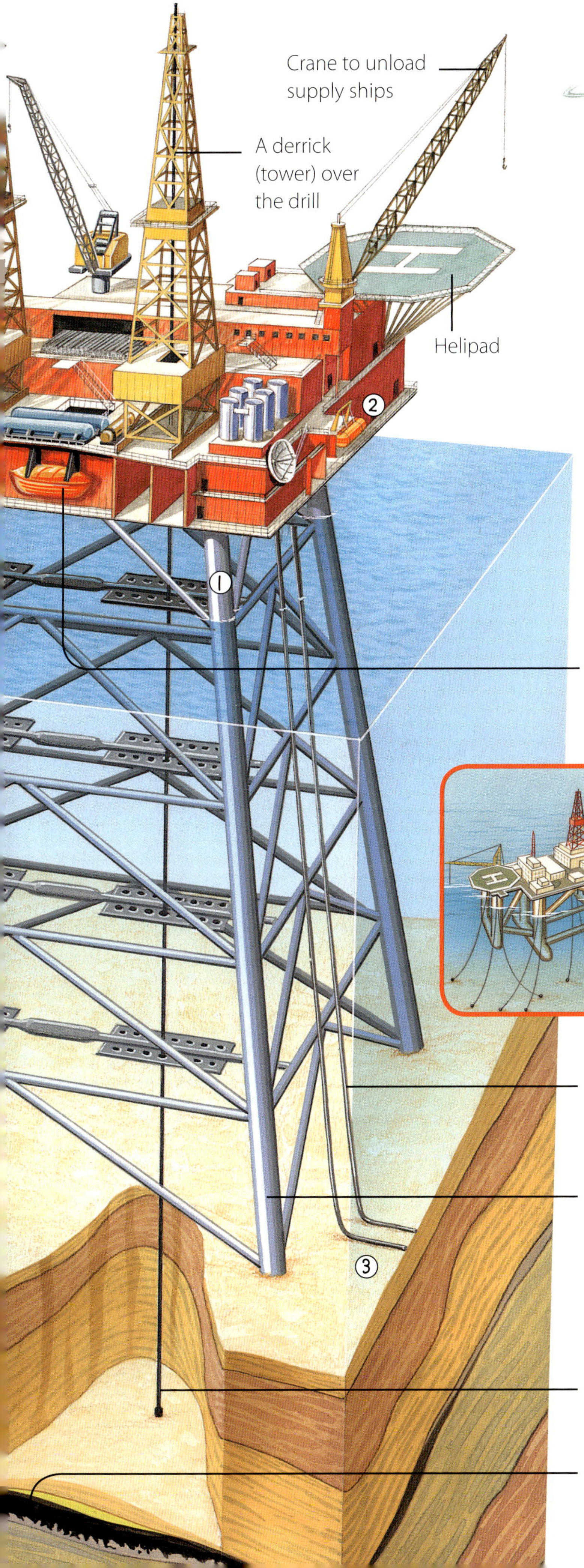

Crane to unload supply ships

A derrick (tower) over the drill

Helipad

Oil production platform

The basic oil production platform consists of a metal jacket or framework (**1**) extending from the sea floor up to a height above the highest possible waves. The superstructure (**2**) is built on top of this framework. This carries all of the equipment needed to safely drill holes in the seabed, draw oil out of the reservoir, carefully control the rate of flow, and pump it either along a pipeline to a shore base (**3**) or load it directly onto oil tankers. The platform is powered by gas turbines (**4**) which provide electricity and pressurise the oil well to get the oil to the surface more quickly.

Gas comes up with the oil – some is injected back into the reservoir, some is used to fuel the turbines, and if there is enough left over it is separated and sent to the shore for use. Any excess is burned off at the end of a long boom (**5**).

Special ifeboats are designed to allow safe escape through seas covered with burning oil

Pipelines carry oil or gas to the shore and other nearby wells

Platform types

As well as the steel jacket rig, other types of drilling platform include: a floating platform held by anchors (*above left*) and used in deep water or for smaller oil fields; a large concrete platform (*above centre*), which is able to withstand severe weather and has storage tanks built into the base; a sea floor wellhead (*above right*), installed by a drilling ship in deep waters and then left in place to automatically pump oil ashore.

The platform is anchored in place with long steel pins

The drill penetrates the oil reservoir

Oil trapped beneath dense rock

Ocean Power

The sea contains huge amounts of energy that will never run out. The power of both waves and tides can be used to generate electricity in ways that do not cause pollution or release gases that can affect the Earth's climate. So why has it taken so long to exploit this vast power source? The answer is that the costs of building and looking after ocean power machinery are high, and though cheap to run, they may impact sea life and are affected by storms and weather damage. Offshore wind farms are now widely used, but they rely on the wind, not the oceans to produce power. As scientists and engineers look for clean alternatives to fossil fuels, many types of projects to harness the power of the oceans are being researched and developed.

Tidal power station

People first made use of sea power by building dams across estuaries. At high tide the estuary would fill up. At low tide the water was released, passing across a water wheel geared to a mill to grind grain. Today, tidal barrage power stations on the Rance river in France (*right*) and at Sihwa Lake in South Korea, use water to spin turbines to make electricity.

Thermal power

Ocean Thermal Energy Conversion (OTEC) uses the difference in temperature between warm surface water and deep cold water to evaporate liquid ammonia and spin a turbine electrical generator. It works best in the tropics where the cold water can be piped to nearby islands after use.

The picture (*right*) shows how the system works. Warm surface water boils liquid ammonia to turn it into a vapour (1). The ammonia vapour spins a turbine to make electricity (2). Very cold water is drawn up from deep in the ocean (3), and condenses the ammonia back into liquid (4). The liquid ammonia travels back to the tank (5) to be used again and again.

Cross-section of a thermal power plant

Cold water (below 5 °C) is drawn up from a depth of over 500 metres

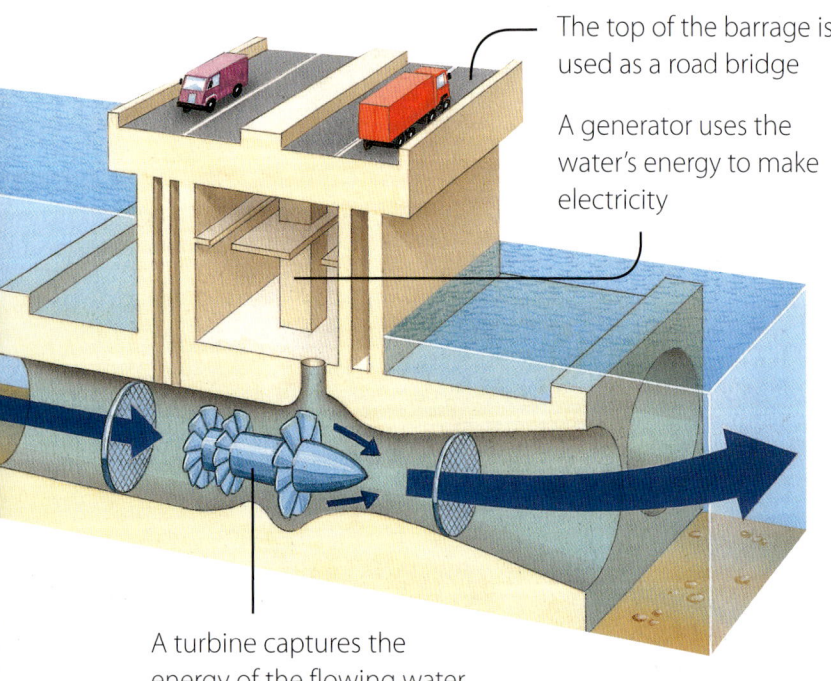

The top of the barrage is used as a road bridge

A generator uses the water's energy to make electricity

A turbine captures the energy of the flowing water

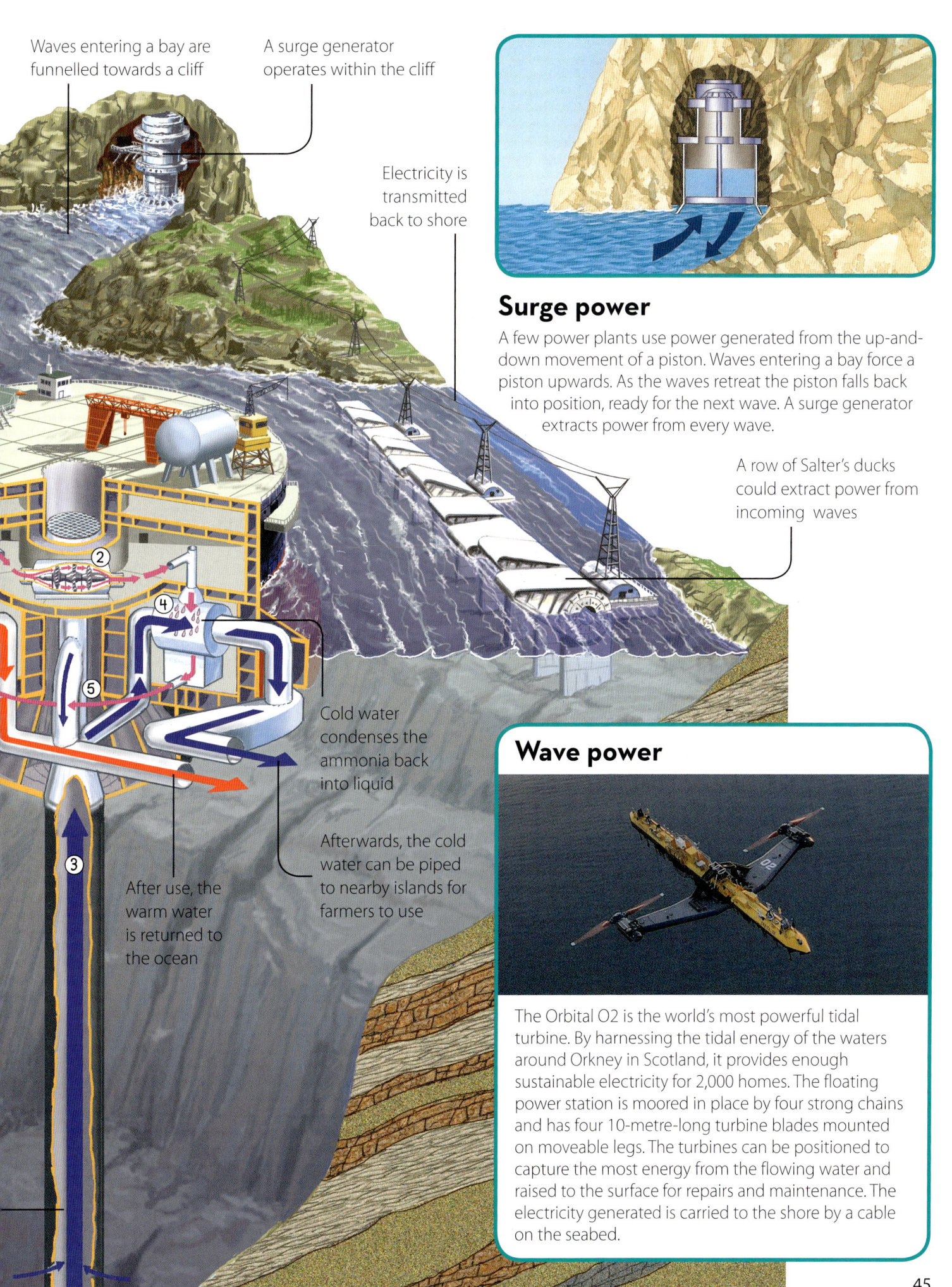

Waves entering a bay are funnelled towards a cliff

A surge generator operates within the cliff

Electricity is transmitted back to shore

A row of Salter's ducks could extract power from incoming waves

Cold water condenses the ammonia back into liquid

After use, the warm water is returned to the ocean

Afterwards, the cold water can be piped to nearby islands for farmers to use

Surge power

A few power plants use power generated from the up-and-down movement of a piston. Waves entering a bay force a piston upwards. As the waves retreat the piston falls back into position, ready for the next wave. A surge generator extracts power from every wave.

Wave power

The Orbital O2 is the world's most powerful tidal turbine. By harnessing the tidal energy of the waters around Orkney in Scotland, it provides enough sustainable electricity for 2,000 homes. The floating power station is moored in place by four strong chains and has four 10-metre-long turbine blades mounted on moveable legs. The turbines can be positioned to capture the most energy from the flowing water and raised to the surface for repairs and maintenance. The electricity generated is carried to the shore by a cable on the seabed.

Index

A
abyssal zone 33
albatross 37
Alvin 28–29
angelfish 38, 39
animals *see* life
Antarctic 14, 15, 36
Arctic 14, 15
atolls, coral 39
auk 36

B
Ballard, Dr Robert 30
ballistic missiles 24–25
barnacles 34
Beaufort Scale 10
birds 35, 36–37
booby 37
breathing apparatus 26
burrowing on beach 34
butterfly fish 38

C
charts 17
chemical pollution 40, 41
clams 38
clownfish 38
coast 12–13
   life 34–35
computer models 17
continental shelf 6, 7
coral reefs 7, 38–39
cormorant 37
Cousteau, Jacques 26
crabs 35
crown-of-thorns 38
currents, ocean 11, 14

D
deposition, coastal 13
diving
   scuba 26–27
   submarine 25
   submersible 28–29
   suit 29
   for wrecks 31
dumping at sea 41

E
erosion, coastal 12–13

F
factory ship 22–23
fertiliser damage 40
fish 9, 14, 23, 32–33, 38–39
fishing 22–23
food chains 33
frozen seas 14–15

G
gas 42
giant tube worms 32
gills 33
glaciers 14–15
grab sampler 17
grouper 38
guillemot 37

H
hand signals by divers 27
Hass, Hans 26
helicopter 42
hot water vents 32

I
icebergs 15
icebreakers 14, 18, 19
islands 7

K
kittiwake 37

L
life (plants and animals) 32–33
   coastal 34–35
   coral reefs 38–39
   floor of ocean 17
   frozen seas 14
   seabirds 35, 36–37
   and tides 9
limpets 9, 35
liner, cruise 20–21
lionfish 39
loggerhead turtle 34
longshore drift 13
lugworm 34

M
mangroves 35
mapping sea 16–17
mining in sea 42–43
mining, waste from 41
Moon and tides 8–9
mudskipper 35

N
navigation 21
neap tides 8, 9
nets 23
nuclear power 19
nuclear weapons 24

O
oceanic rock 6
oceanographer 16
oil platform 42–43
oil slicks 41

P
pelican, brown 36
penguin 37
petrel, storm 36
plankton 14, 17, 32, 33, 36, 40
   poisonous 40, 41
plants *see* life
plates 6, 7
poison 39, 40–41
pollution, ocean 40–41
polyp, coral 38, 39
power from ocean 44–45
propellers 21
puffin 37

R
razors 34
ROVs (remotely operated
   vehicles) 30–31

S
sand gaper 34
satellite navigation 21
scuba diving 26–27
sea cucumbers 32, 38
sea mouse 34
sea potato 34
sea slaters 35
sea urchins 35
seabirds 35, 36–37
seasons 15
seaweed 9, 34, 35
sewage dumped 40, 41
shellfish 9, 35, 38
ships
   early 18–19
   icebreakers 14, 19
   modern 20–21
   pollution 41
   research 16–17
shipwrecks 30–31, 41
sonar 16, 23, 25, 30
splash zone 34
spring tides 8, 9
stabilisers 20–21
starfish 35, 38
storms 10–11
submarines 24–25
submersibles 28–29
Sun and tides 8–9
sunlit zone 33
surge power 45

T
temperature of ocean 11
thermal power 44–45
tides 8–9
   power from 44–45
Titanic 18, 19, 29, 30
treasure 30
Trieste 28
tube worms 32
twilight zone 32

V
volcanoes 6, 7, 39

W
waste, pollution by 40–41
waves 10–11, 12, 13
   power from 45
wetsuits 27
whale 14, 31, 33
wind 10, 14, 15, 18